HIV
LAW

HIV LAW

A Survival Guide to the Legal System for People Living with HIV

Paul Hampton Crockett

THREE RIVERS PRESS • NEW YORK

Although the incidents described in the examples illustrating the book actually occurred, the names of the people involved and certain other facts have been changed in order to protect their privacy.

Copyright © 1997 by Paul Hampton Crockett

All rights reserved. No part of this book may be reproduced or transmitted in any form or by any means, electronic or mechanical, including photocopying, recording, or by any information storage and retrieval system, without permission in writing from the publisher.

Published by Three Rivers Press, a division of Crown Publishers, Inc., 201 East 50th Street, New York, New York 10022. Member of the Crown Publishing Group.
http://www.randomhouse.com/
Random House, Inc. New York, Toronto, London, Sydney, Auckland
THREE RIVERS PRESS and colophon are trademarks of
Crown Publishers, Inc.

Printed in the United States of America

Design by Leonard Henderson

Library of Congress Cataloging-in-Publication Data is available upon request.

ISBN 0-609-80023-X

10 9 8 7 6 5 4 3 2

*In celebration of the life of
Scott R. Gillen,
whose love transforms me still*

CONTENTS

Acknowledgments **8**
Introduction **10**
1. Why Do You Need a Will or Trust?   15
   What You Need to Know About Wills   15
   A Little About Trusts   23
2. Are You Aware of What You Have . . . and How You Are Holding It?   29
3. Are You Sure About How You Are Holding Title to Your Home?   34
4. What You Need to Know About Guardianship   38
   Guardianship for Children   42
5. Using Powers of Attorney   45
6. You and Your Bank Accounts   50
7. Planning for Your Health Care Needs: Naming Your Health Care Proxy   55
8. Thinking About Your Living Will   59
   "Do Not Resuscitate" (DNR) Orders   61
9. Navigating the Quicksands: How to Safeguard Your Documents Against Attack   63
10. Introduction to Insurance Issues: Covering the Basics   69
    Some Important Definitions   73
    A Few Points on Life Insurance Coverage   78

Disability Insurance: A Look at the Basics 79
Confidentiality and Insurance 85
11. Focus on Health Insurance: Access to Coverage and Quality of Care in Changing Times 92
The 1996 Federal Health Insurance Reforms: Where Do You Now Fit into the Picture? 94
On Keeping Your Health Insurance and Your COBRA Rights 104
More Ways to Keep Covered 111
The Challenge of Managed Care 120
12. The World According to Social Security: What You Need to Know 128
A Look at the Social Security Appeals Process 144
13. Dealing with Creditors: A Look at Some Alternatives to Bankruptcy 151
14. The Basics of Bankruptcy 160
15. Selling Your Life Insurance 164
16. Discrimination: What Are Your Rights? 185
Focus on the "Americans with Disabilities" Act 187
17. A Survival Guide to HIV in the Workplace 194
Know Your Rights under the Family Medical Leave Act 197
Conclusion 201
Appendix A: Glossary of Terms 202
Appendix B: Resources for Further Information and Access to Legal Representation 212
Index 231

ACKNOWLEDGMENTS

Though the name on this book may be mine alone, a great many people have over the years helped inspire me, challenge me, teach me, and coach and encourage me through the rough times. Without them, this book would not have been possible. Most of the examples illustrating this book flow directly from the real-life experiences of my clients, friends, and lovers as they have risen to the awesome challenges posed by HIV. Through their example, I have learned great lessons of life, death, and what it means to be human.

No words are adequate to capture the horror of AIDS, and no means exist to sound the depths of our collective loss. Even against the ominous backdrop of the suffering and the death, however, we have been given the opportunity to learn great lessons. From those battling the illness, we have learned what it means to really treasure life. I am grateful to those who have allowed me to share their battle. They have taught me the true meaning of courage, dignity, and humor. They have enriched me by showing me victories of the human spirit.

This book is an ambitious project, and I must thank the experts who agreed to review and assist me with certain chapters. On the social security chapter, I appreciate the input of attorney Clint Hurst, a specialist in social security appeals, and Carl M. Galli of the Social Security Administration, the HIV-benefits coordinator for the South Miami Beach office. I also thank attorney Doug Snyder of Miami, Florida, for his important contributions to the bankruptcy chapter. On the insurance chapters, I acknowledge the excellent ideas and assistance of attorney Mark Scherzer of New York, as well as attorney Byron Mathews of Miami, Florida, and financial adviser Per Larson of New York. The ideas and the editorial contributions of all of these people were invaluable. If errors remain in the text, blame them on me. After all, they tried!

I also appreciate the assistance of Cliff Cortez and the staff at the office of the American Bar Association AIDS Coordinating Committee in helping to put together the national resource directory, appendix B to this book.

I thank my "soul sister," Daviea Serbin Davis, of Pittsburgh, Pennsylvania, whose love and ongoing support have helped me pick up the pieces and continue to heal following the death of my hero and my true love, Scott Richard Gillen, of AIDS on March 1, 1996.

I thank my law partner, Jerry Simon Chasen, for his ongoing support and his commitment to protecting the legal rights of people living with HIV, and my former partner, Gary S. Franklin, for his support while I was working on this project. I must also recognize the contributions of my friends Richard C. Milstein, who first taught me to practice law, and Bill Adams, who several years ago led me to give my first lecture on AIDS and the law and shared his outline to help me do so. I am also grateful to the many fine and dedicated people I have been privileged to work with through the Health Crisis Network in Miami, Florida over the years. They love people, hate AIDS, and fight tirelessly.

I also acknowledge a debt of gratitude to my agent, Jed Mattes, without whose help this book would probably never have made it into your hands.

Finally, I cannot express deeply enough my gratitude to my family. Through it all, they have been there for me and have never wavered in their love and support. I am grateful.

INTRODUCTION

An HIV diagnosis changes everything.

Once you have gotten that news, life can sometimes feel as if you have stepped "through the looking glass." Although the world itself has not changed, everything seems completely different, and the old rules just do not apply. Only those faced with a life-threatening illness truly understand the significance of access to health care, and the pressures raised by dealing with a chronic health condition in a system dominated by (often) adversarial insurance providers and government bureaucracies.

Life with HIV raises a host of other challenges, among them psychological/social, financial, and legal issues. People are often forced to face these awesome challenges without a lot of guidance or social support, and as HIV continues its slow and steady burn into America's communities, still hitting especially hard its minority groups, new and complex challenges are being raised daily. HIV has for too long been viewed as "someone else's problem," affecting primarily gays, racial minorities, IV-drug users, and now, increasingly, women and children. Many have come to recognize the terrible reality of the epidemic only when someone they love is affected.

Never before has our society been confronted with anything like HIV. Even now, when we may yet have seen only the tip of the iceberg of this epidemic, many of our social institutions are already being stretched to the breaking point. Individually and as a society, we are being forced into uncharted waters.

Second only to the medical issues raised by HIV, legal issues take prominence in the lives of those dealing with the disease. At virtually every stage of the process, new legal issues arise and cry out for resolution. What is "disability," and what benefits are available to me? Who's got the right to know about my positive test results? Can they fire me if they find out? How can I keep my health insurance? Can I really sell my life insurance policy? What will happen to my property if I die? Who will take care of the kids? Should I declare bankruptcy? What actions can I take to protect those I love?

The questions go on and on, infinite in number and unique to each situation. Nevertheless, it is important to realize that legal protections are available to all Americans with HIV, and every state has laws in place to protect our rights. Why is it so important to understand what they are? Because we must face head-on the homophobia, racism, sexism, and other dark undercurrents that make our society what it is and put people with HIV at special risk. Preparing for the future must start with a genuine effort to accurately assess the possible pitfalls that await if we fail to plan ahead.

Those pitfalls can be devastating. Although the law provides means for each of us to decide whom we would like to make health care decisions for us if we become unable to do so, to receive our property once we have died, to serve as our guardian, or to follow through with our funeral wishes, those rights are often lost if not acted upon. Then the law dictates who has priority, setting the stage for powerful and intense battles. In every case, regardless of your wishes, the law will bestow these rights on blood relations. Whether you are gay or straight, that may not be what you would have wanted to happen.

Although it is not easy to face up to the difficult issues raised by the prospect of death and disability so as to effectively plan ahead, it is definitely worth it. In my law practice, I have found that "taking the bull by the horns" often helps to empower the client. Although an HIV diagnosis can at times raise some issues beyond a client's control, a real feeling of pride and well-being can result from our assurance that we have done everything possible to protect ourselves and those we love.

The purpose of this book is to present a "nutshell" guide to some of the key legal issues raised by HIV, and to offer some guidance through that maze. Our goal has been to present, for perhaps the first time under one cover, up-to-date and accurate information on the broad range of practical legal problems confronting people with HIV.

This book is not intended to be academic in nature, nor a complete treatise on all aspects of HIV and the law. Instead, recognizing that people with HIV are frequently confronted with difficult and important choices, on which decisions must be made quickly, this book is intended to serve as a "survival guide." If one continuous theme runs through the book, it is that people with HIV must often fight to get what is rightfully theirs. In a number of ways, and for a number of reasons, contemporary America is not an easy or supportive place for people with HIV to live. To get what you need, you may have to insist upon your rights or fight for them, and you may not prevail unless you have armed yourself with knowledge. That is where this book comes in.

A Time of Flux

It has been a real challenge to bring you up-to-date with accurate information, as we live in a time of rapid flux. First, important treatment breakthroughs are now being made, providing hope that HIV is already becoming a chronic and manageable illness rather than a terminal one. The advent of protease inhibitors, the apparent effectiveness of combination drug "cocktails" to fight the virus, and advances in our basic scientific understanding of how the virus works all offer real hope for the future. In the meantime, these advances have already had a dramatic impact on the previously booming viatical industry (the companies that purchase life insurance policies as an investment), and have started to cast into question long-established assumptions about HIV-related disability, both in private coverage and through the Social Security Administration. Sick and disabled people are now recovering their health, and that rarely used to happen.

Important federal legislation passed in 1996 has also dramatically changed many areas of the law important to people with HIV. The Health Insurance Portability and Accountability Act of 1996 focuses primarily on health insurance reform in both the group and individual markets and takes effect (for the most part) after July 1, 1997. The legislation strikes a blow at "job lock" and enhances portability of coverage by severely limiting exclusion periods for preexisting conditions, guarantees availability and renewability of group coverage, and even requires "guaranteed issue" of individual coverage if you meet a number of conditions. The law also somewhat simplifies access to the extra eleven months of COBRA continuation coverage available to you if you have left your job because of disability. (As we'll explore in chapter 11, COBRA is a federal law forcing some employers to allow you to keep your group insurance coverage in place for certain periods of time even though you have left the job.) Additionally, the law exempts the proceeds of some viatical settlement transactions from federal taxes.

Further, significantly, the law encourages the states to seek out their own creative solutions to the challenge of access to health care. Hopefully, the law will stimulate progress and a national dialogue on that issue.

A FEW NOTES ABOUT USING THIS BOOK

First, please realize that laws often vary from state to state, and it is important that you check out the specifics of your state's laws before you take important actions. The information contained in this book should point you in the right direction, but is not intended to replace the assistance of an attorney or other appropriate adviser on your specific matter. Accordingly, we have included in appendix B to this book some resources that might either provide or lead you toward legal advice or representation, no matter where you might live in the country.

Sometimes it may not be easy to get the right assistance, especially when funds are limited, but don't give up without trying. Even if you have no money, pro bono (free) or reduced-price services may be available as a result of your HIV status—check it out. No matter what your HIV status, you have certain basic rights, but the burden falls on you to ensure that those rights are not lost.

Use your common sense when interviewing a lawyer you may be working with on your matter. Do not hesitate to ask the attorney specific questions about his or her experience in the area in which you need help, ask how much it will cost you, and honor your instincts if you feel that the attorney is not right for you. It may be a good idea to consult with two or three attorneys before making your decision.

Protect yourself! Before hiring an attorney, applying for benefits, or taking any other important steps, do your homework and know your rights.

One final note: the law in this area changes rapidly. For updates and current information, visit the author's Web site on the Internet at http://www.HIVLawToday.com.

1

Why Do You Need a Will or Trust?

Why is it so important that you plan ahead and put into place an estate plan that is right for you? Are estate plans only for rich people? What are some of the basic options available to you? What can happen if you fail to plan ahead and take action? How might the system be stacked against you?

While these questions are important for everyone, it can be especially dangerous for people with HIV to leave them unanswered. We'll now take a look at the two basic options available to you in putting together an estate plan: *wills* and *trusts*. Hopefully, you will then have enough basic information to begin thinking about which alternative might be right for you.

What You Need to Know About Wills

The good news is that under the law you have an absolute right to decide who is to inherit your property after your death, to name the person you would like to have in charge of your estate (called your executor or personal representative, depending on your state), and to choose the type of funeral and burial arrangements that are right for you. The bad news is that you must use these rights or lose them. That is where your will comes in.

This is the problem: if you do not exercise your right to make a will or otherwise plan ahead, your life partner, close friends, or other chosen individuals will be left out in the cold and the law will dictate who gets your property. Many people outside the mainstream, whether gay or unmarried straight people, have learned the hard way that the law does not recognize the validity (or even the existence) of their relationships for purposes of inheritance and related issues. If you die leaving no will, the law will not care that you were in a long-term relationship or that your best friend could really have used the money or that you might have liked to leave something to AIDS charities.

Instead, the law will distribute your property in the following priority (check your state's laws on this, as they may vary): (a) your *spouse* (warning: since gays cannot legally marry one another, this does *not* include your lover! Also, in most states this *does not* include your life partner of the opposite sex if you are not legally married, no matter how long you have been together); (b) your *children;* (c) your *parents;* (d) your *brothers and sisters* and *their children;* (e) your *grandparents,* then *aunts and uncles,* etc. While the law probably works fairly well for the majority of our society, who are presumed by the law to be both straight *and* married, it may not necessarily work for you. Be aware.

What are the legal requirements of a will? Fairly simple, but *extremely* important. Again, do not leave this to guesswork: be certain about the requirements of your state. Most states require wills to be in writing (whether typed or handwritten) and witnessed by at least two adults. This is too important to leave to guesswork: find out exactly what the laws of your state require!

Although not required to be legally effective, the will should be notarized by a notary public who has attended the will signing. Gay people, and others who can anticipate a hassle from surviving family members, need to take special precautions to safeguard their wills, and the advice of an attorney is strongly recommended. The cost of a slip-up is too high.

> I once consulted with a man whose life partner of sixteen years had died a few days before. In real distress, he ex-

plained that his lover's family was becoming more and more abusive, even threatening to force him from the home he and his lover had shared for over ten years. I asked, "Whose name was the house in?" When he said, "My lover's," my heart sank. "But there's a will," he said, and pulled it out of his pocket. Unfortunately, the will was witnessed by only one person and was therefore a useless piece of paper under Florida law. I had to sit down and explain to him that notwithstanding their long-term relationship, and even though his lover's intention had been clear, the law would vest title to the home in the lover's family. All for the failure of one signature; all because his lover had wanted to "get by" without consulting an attorney. What had he saved in the long run?

Too often, a family's grief and rage at premature death can turn into a legal vendetta against a surviving life partner. In one case, a survivor returned from his lover's funeral to find that his lover's family had taken from the home the valuable collection of antiques the couple had accumulated during their years together, and even some of their nicer kitchenware. In another case, a woman's sizable estate was claimed by her parents after her death because she had "never gotten around" to making the will that would have fulfilled her desire to protect her long-term boyfriend. Although her parents never seemed to care about her while she was alive, they certainly became interested in her property once she had passed away! Time and again, survivors left alone by an AIDS death have found themselves on the wrong side of a law that can be harsh. Please do not let it happen to you.

Be aware of two common pitfalls.

First, many people think that wills are only necessary for the rich. Not so. Even if your estate is not huge, whatever you have worked hard to earn, acquire, and save should go to the people of your choice. If you want to leave your property to your parents or other blood relations, fine, but if you have other plans, you had better act on them!

Second, people are often lulled into a false sense of security by thinking that "those problems aren't going to happen to me, my lover's parents are cool." Beware. No one knows exactly how anyone in extreme grief or anger will react, and the prospect of "free money" can make people crazy. In gay situations, previously suppressed homophobia can sometimes explosively mix with a parent's feeling of entitlement to create a nasty situation. Too often, in their heart of hearts parents don't *really* understand or respect gay relationships and feel on a gut level that any property acquired by their child during his or her lifetime should go "back to the family" after the child's death.

In situations involving people of the opposite sex, too, blood relations of the deceased sometimes tend to devalue the relationship in the absence of formal marriage. Keep your eyes open.

As Mark Twain warned, you don't really know someone until you have inherited with them.

So, beyond determining who gets your property, what else can a will do?

First, you can name the person whom you would like to serve as the *executor* or *personal representative* of your estate. Since the person you name will assume responsibility for gathering assets, paying creditors, distributing to beneficiaries, and will of necessity be privy to all information relating to your estate, it is important that you name someone you trust. Battles have sometimes erupted between gay survivors and the parents or other blood-family members of the deceased over the question of who is to act as the administrator of the estate. If there is no will, guess who will be out of luck? Parents and other blood relations are almost always given priority under the law, unless you have legally provided to the contrary.

It is also important that you state in your will your wishes as to the disposition of your body, such as cremation or burial, and funeral arrangements. Don't leave your survivors wondering about what you would have wanted. Although it is better to make preneed arrangements if you anticipate a conflict on this issue, having stated your wishes in your will should help to place your chosen administrator in a position of authority should a problem arise. And again, conflicts have arisen on these questions. Let's take a look at an example:

> A few months ago, I received a call from Marcia, who explained that Dan, the man she had been living with for almost ten years, was hospitalized and near death. Although Dan had made clear his desire that his remains be cremated and disposed of at sea, his family strongly objected. As Dan lay ill, they told Marcia that "no matter what, our son will be buried in the family plot" in upstate New York. Unfortunately, one of Dan's real concerns during his last days was that his wish to be cremated would not be carried out.
>
> Fortunately, although he was extremely ill, Dan was mentally capable at that time. Accordingly, I suggested that he enter into a preneed contract with a cremation service to remove all doubt as to his desires. He contacted a local cremation service and signed and paid for a binding contract directing that his remains be cremated, and that the ashes be delivered to Marcia rather than his family for handling. Those were his wishes.
>
> Marcia recently called to inform me that Dan had passed away, but that his contract had given him a great deal of peace of mind in his last days.

So what is the lesson here? As is typical, Dan had an absolute right to make the basic decision for himself as to the disposition of his remains, the type of funeral, etc. Had he not taken the action to protect his wishes, though, his family would automatically have taken legal priority over Marcia in making those decisions and could have taken her to court on those issues. Also, even if the family had been agreeable to cremation, a dispute could have arisen over the distribution of the ashes. The contract took care of that.

Keep in mind, too, that Dan could have also specified his wishes in his will, or even in a separate written statement. Because he had not, though, the contract was the way to go.

One final note: Although it does not hurt to state your wishes as to cremation and burial in a power-of-attorney document (see chapter 5), the problem is that such documents, technically, expire upon your death. It is a better idea to state your wishes in your will, but your best bet is to sign a contract in advance. Though it may be tough for you, think of it as a major gift you are leaving to your survivors.

Finally, another important function of a will, if you are a parent of minor children, is to state your wishes as to a guardian for them in the event of your death. In some states, you can accomplish the same goal by signing another document, specifically naming the person(s) you would like to be responsible for your children (see chapter 4), but stating your wishes in your will will not hurt.

As you can see, making your will is extremely important, and absolute disaster can result for your survivors if you fail to do so. You must also be aware, though, that your will may be attacked by greedy or spiteful relatives. Particularly when HIV is involved, precautions should be taken to safeguard the validity of your will and other important documents.

In chapter 9, we'll take a look at some of the common grounds on which wills are attacked and explore strategy to protect yourself against those challenges. Now, let's look at a classic example of how *not* to do your estate planning:

> Fernando and Walter, both HIV-positive, were lovers for eight years before Fernando was diagnosed with AIDS.

After repeated struggles with various illnesses and opportunistic infections, Fernando continued to decline. Walter and Fernando shared a comfortable relationship with Fernando's parents, who lived in California and who had visited once or twice in the past. After Walter called the parents, they flew in from the West Coast to say good-bye to their son and to do what they could.

Not until Fernando literally lay on death's door did he and Walter realize that he had made no will or other estate plan, and that if they failed to act, his parents would have the right to their house, which was in Fernando's name, and to the rest of Fernando's property. Horrified, Walter rushed out to an office supply store and bought a bunch of legal forms, including a will. By that point, Fernando had lost motor coordination for part of his body and was unable to fill in the blanks on the will, to write his wishes, or to sign a recognizable signature.

Accordingly, Walter filled in the will himself, making himself the beneficiary, and the parents signed as witnesses to their son's scrawled signature on the will. Walter and Fernando breathed a sigh of relief, and Fernando died shortly thereafter with at least some peace of mind. After his death, the body was cremated and Walter flew out of town for an appointment with an out-of-state AIDS clinic. Before he left, he offered the parents the use of his home, as well as his car.

When Walter returned, the home had been ransacked, with papers spread out all over, and certain items missing. Before he could speak with Fernando's family, he got a call from an attorney the parents had hired to help them "break the will" and to "get what was rightfully theirs." While Walter had been out of town getting treatment, the parents had inventoried the contents of the home and made a list. On top of the grief at losing his lover, Walter was in shock at these events.

After Walter retained us as his attorneys, we began dealing with the other lawyer, who said with a sneer in his voice, "We both know how the law views these kinds of relationships." The parents demanded several items from the home, including books, art, and antique furniture. Because Walter's health was shaky, and the cost of the battle was not worth the hassle to him, a compromise agreement was reached. Walter is happy because he will keep the home. Unfortunately, though, the stress he has had to live through can never be undone.

What are the important lessons to be learned from the above scenario?

Don't wait until the last minute. Particularly when you are dealing with HIV infection, the longer you wait to deal with it and get an estate plan in place, and the more advanced the disease, the greater the odds that the will can successfully be attacked on the grounds that you were too sick to understand what you were doing when you signed it.

Don't try to do it yourself. As tempting as it might be to try to save a buck by doing it yourself instead of seeing a lawyer, it is well worth it to pay what it costs. If you are working, no matter what your job, you can probably afford to have a lawyer help you prepare a will. (Just ask an attorney how much he or she would charge; it might be less than you think.) If you don't pay now, the person or people you love might pay much more later.

If you cannot afford to pay a lawyer full price, don't assume that you will be unable to find one to work with you, at least without trying. If you are low on funds and have HIV, you might be able to get free or reduced-price legal help on that basis. Take a look at legal resources listed in appendix B to this book, and see if you can find a local resource to help you out or point you in the right direction.

On the other hand, if you can afford to pay an attorney to do your plan, even if you need to do so in installments, move on it *now*. It is probably the best money you are likely to spend, and especially if you are in a nontraditional relationship (of whatever kind), you could be saving your significant other from likely legal hassles and possible financial ruin.

Think about it.

Be aware of "undue influence" claims. More than any other factor, Fernando's will was weakened by the fact that Walter himself wrote it out. After all, the transaction had the appearance of Walter writing himself a check from Fernando's account! (What cues would indicate to a judge reviewing this situation that the will was actually Fernando's project and not Walter's, even though Fernando's name was on it?) Be aware that one of the most frequent attacks on wills is "undue influence," meaning that the will is invalid because it does not truly reflect the wishes of the person signing the will and has been made as a result of unreasonable pressure or persuasion applied by another person (see chapter 9). Be very careful about *any* direct involvement in the making or signing of your partner's will, and let an experienced attorney guide you through the process.

A LITTLE ABOUT TRUSTS

Depending on your situation, trusts can open up a range of possibilities in planning that may otherwise not be open to you. Many types of trusts are available, which serve many purposes, but the most useful for most people, and commonly used, is the living trust or inter vivos revocable trust. Don't let the Latin scare you; trusts can be very user friendly and in some ways are beautifully suited to the special needs of people with HIV. Whether or not you have substantial assets, you may find that a living trust meets your planning needs.

What Is a Trust?

To put it simply, a trust is a legal creation that you set up by signing a trust document. In the document, you name the person you would like to have serve as "trustee" (the person in charge of the assets), which can be yourself. You can also name a "successor trustee," who will be able to take over management of the assets in the event you become disabled. Obviously, this is often a key concern for people with HIV. Finally, you can dictate within the trust whom you would like to inherit your property after your death. By doing so, you can often make inheritance quicker and more secure for your heirs and make things a little more difficult for any creditors you might leave behind.

Here is a helpful analogy: think of a trust as a big shopping bag. You take your home, other real estate owned by you, your bank accounts, brokerage accounts, etc., and put them into the bag and tie it up. Once that has been done, you are still the owner of the property, but title to the property is now held in the name of the trust. The property is securely held "in the bag." What difference does that make? Let's look at an example:

> Elsa sets up a living trust, naming herself as the trustee. She provides in the trust that her boyfriend, Boris, is to take over management of her assets in the event she becomes incapacitated. The trust provides that after her death, her assets will be available to Boris for his lifetime and will then pass to an AIDS charity after his death. She also signs a "pour over" will, which serves as a safety net to make sure that any assets she may have failed to transfer to the trust by the time of her death will "pour [back] over" into the trust after her estate has been administered.
>
> To give effect to the trust, she signs deeds conveying ownership of her two homes from her own name to "Elsa

> Addams, as Trustee of the Elsa Addams Trust, dated October 31, 1996." She similarly changes the title to all of her bank and brokerage accounts, stock holdings, etc. Once everything has been transferred into the trust, Elsa is still fully in control of her assets. She feels as secure as possible, however, that she and those she loves will be protected in the event of her incapacity or death.

For any plan to work successfully, as a whole, it is *essential* that the trust be "funded," meaning that you must take the steps necessary to transfer your assets into the trust. (In the analogy above, that's when you put your property "into the bag.") If you fail to follow through on that, the trust will be a useless document because its terms will have nothing to apply to! A trust can only serve its intended purposes to the extent you have put your assets under its control.

Let's look at another example, without such a happy ending:

> Ian is an educated consumer who has heard about the benefits of estate planning with trusts. After he becomes ill, he realizes that he has no estate plan in place and decides to have a trust drawn up. He consolidates various bank and brokerage accounts into one account, with the intention of transferring title from the current "Ian Smith" to "Ian Smith, Trustee of the Ian Smith Revocable Trust dated 11/7/96." He then signs a trust naming his dear friend Shirley to replace him as trustee if he ever becomes incapacitated, and setting forth his wishes for the disposition of his property in the event of his death.
>
> Unfortunately, he never gets around to retitling the account. As a result, Shirley is unable to get to the funds for his benefit after he becomes incapacitated, and after his death the account is still in his name, necessitating an ex-

pensive probate administration in court to gain access to the funds. To make matters worse, his intended beneficiaries are not able to get to the funds for several months after his death, attorneys' fees mount up during the administration of the estate, and all of his creditors must be given a chance to file claims before any money is distributed to beneficiaries.

Remember, "funding" is key when it comes to making trusts serve their purpose. Ian's intent was frustrated because he failed to follow through on this crucial aspect of the trust process.

Do You Need a Trust?

Is a trust the right estate-planning tool for you? It all depends. To the extent your situation is more complicated than ordinary (and aren't they all!), and you want more long-term control than might be possible with a will, a trust might be right for you. Used creatively, trusts offer a flexibility that can help you plan effectively both for incapacity and for disposition after your death. When might planning with a trust be especially appropriate?

- If you are *running an ongoing business* and it is important to you that the business keep going after your death, you are more likely to reach that goal successfully through a trust rather than a will. By thinking matters through carefully and designating and training key people in your business, you may be able to preserve what you have built up and protect those you love.
- If you *own real property in a state other than the one in which you live,* a trust can be extremely helpful in avoiding expensive and problematic probate proceedings in the other state. Even if an estate proceeding in court is opened for you in your state, that court will *not* have jurisdiction to clear title to the real property

in the other state, and a separate "long distance" (or "ancillary") probate proceeding will be required to deal with that property. It is expensive and it is a hassle. Avoid this if you can.
- If you have *assets approaching or exceeding $600,000* (which, by the way, includes the full value of any life insurance on your life, even though it passes to your named beneficiary outside of probate), you may benefit from tax-sensitive planning using trusts, with or without charitable components. Although trusts do not per se reduce estate-tax liabilities, certain options helpful in limiting estate-tax liabilities may be open to you, especially if you are married.

Finally, HIV infection raises a very real (albeit horrifying) possibility that you might become either physically or mentally unable to manage your own affairs. Trusts work beautifully in this situation because you have (1) consolidated your assets into one form of ownership, making them easier to manage, and (2) you have named a "successor trustee," who is hopefully familiar with your needs and ready to step in and begin handling your affairs if you ever need help. As you can imagine, incapacity is always stressful, and having in place a trust, and a successor trustee, can greatly reduce stress and make a difficult time that much smoother. In the trust, you can define for yourself the starting point of incapacity.

Let's look at an example:

> Bob and Ted are both HIV-positive and have been in a relationship for many years. Both have been ill. Bob is substantially more wealthy than Ted, and he is concerned about protecting both Ted and Bob's elderly mother, Carol. He creates a trust naming himself as the trustee, and his good friend Alice agrees to serve as successor trustee in the event Bob becomes incapacitated. Under the terms of the trust, Alice is to take over as successor trustee when both Bob's

longtime physician and another named individual agree that he is no longer able to manage his affairs and needs help. The trust also provides that, after Bob's death, the trustee is to pay for all of Ted's and Carol's living expenses, plus provide them both with a little cash, for as long as they each should live. After both Ted and Carol have died, the trust funds are to be released to an AIDS-related charity to be chosen by Alice.

ANOTHER SIGNIFICANT ADVANTAGE OF TRUSTS

After your death, no court probate is required, so your beneficiaries are more likely to get their money faster and more hassle-free. (Depending on the laws of your state, family members of a deceased may not be entitled to notice, and a right to contest a trust, whereas they might be if a will were involved. Ask a local attorney about this.) Also, because no court probate is required for trusts, having most or all of your assets pass through the trust can make recovery more difficult for your creditors after your death. Again, you should inquire about your state's laws on this before you act.

THE DOWNSIDE OF TRUSTS

Because they are often more complicated to create and to put into working order than wills, trusts cost a little more in legal fees to set up. You need to decide if that's worth it to you. You must also keep in mind that, depending on the extent of your property, the funding of the trust can be a hassle. Unlike a will, which is completed once it has been properly signed and witnessed, the work of a trustee often only begins once the document is signed.

You, and only you, can decide whether a trust is right for you. But do take a careful look at your situation and think about it!

2

Are You Aware of What You Have . . . and How You Are Holding It?

Yes, wills and trusts are important, but they are only one piece of the puzzle. To put an effective estate plan into place for yourself, one that will really work for you, you must take into careful consideration the kind of real and personal property you own, how you are holding title to that property, and to whom you would like that property to pass after your death. Depending on your situation and your desires, you may have a great range of possibilities in planning open to you.

First, think about what kind of property you own. Take the time to make a list. Here are some common types: your home or other real estate, bank accounts, brokerage or stock accounts, any other financial investments, life insurance policies, retirement plans, ownership interest in a business, frequent flier miles, automobiles, boats, artwork, other collectibles, jewelry, and all of your other "stuff" (or personal property). If you add it all up, you may be worth more than you would have thought.

Making a list of your property is the first step. Then you need to ask yourself what would happen to the property in the event of your death, distinguishing between property that could easily be transferred to others (such as personal property without a title, such as your stereo equipment), property requiring an "official" change of ownership through title or deed (such as real property, cars, boats, etc.), and money or other investments held in banks or other financial institutions. (We'll look at bank account planning in chapter 6.)

If you have thought it through, it is easy enough to put a plan in place for all of the above. To understand the full range of possibilities in simple and effective estate planning, you must understand what wills do, and their limits.

The purpose of a will is to direct distribution of the property owned by you after your death, specifically property held in your own name. *That does not include* for example

- property held jointly by you and someone else, or held *with rights of survivorship* (we'll discuss that later).
- property you have effectively given away during your life.
- life insurance proceeds or retirement accounts (unless you specifically name your estate as the beneficiary, they go directly to the named person).
- bank accounts you have designated "in trust for" another person.

Through the use of devices such as these, you can avoid probate and sometimes even avoid the need for planning through a trust. Your guiding principle should always be "simpler is better." The challenge sometimes is to understand and to weigh the possibilities open to you, then to figure out the simplest solution *that will work for you.*

What does it mean to "avoid probate?" Good question.

Probate is the administration of an estate in court after death, including filing the will with the court if one has been done, having a personal representative or executor appointed by a judge, notifying and paying creditors, if appropriate, and distributing the estate to the beneficiaries.

The two main reasons you will want to avoid probate are attorney's fees and delay. Especially if litigation is involved, probate can be long and complicated. The other major downside of probate is that creditors may have the right to have their claims paid from the estate before your heirs can receive their due.

If you have transferred your property out of your own name prior to your death, however, your creditors will be out of luck, even if their claims against you are legitimate. If you have seen to it that the well of your estate is dry, nothing will be available for your creditors and they will have little incentive to try for it.

Consider the following examples. To avoid probate:

> Janice has the title to her car changed from her name alone to add her boyfriend as co-owner.
>
> Charles names his life partner as the ITF ("In Trust For") beneficiary of his bank account, meaning that Charles alone can draw money from the account while he is alive, but that the funds will automatically pass to his partner should Charles die.
>
> Elizabeth changes the beneficiary of her life insurance policy from "the Estate of Elizabeth" to her husband, resulting in the payment of funds directly to him and bypassing the need for probate.
>
> Although Vicki has almost no money in the bank, she fears that her family will try to take her furniture and silverware after her death. She wants her life partner, Sheila, to inherit everything in the house. Accordingly, in front of respectable, independent witnesses, Vicki makes a gift of all of her property to Sheila. Alternatively, she signs a bill of sale evidencing that Sheila has paid for the property, either with cash or in return for caretaking services rendered to Vicki by Sheila.
>
> And then Vicki changes the locks to her apartment!

By taking such simple actions as the above, the need for opening an estate can sometimes be avoided. The less property you have, the better an idea it might be to consider placing all of your property in joint names. (*Caveat:* if you have a "taxable estate," i.e., more than about $600,000 in assets, disastrous tax consequences can result from holding your property jointly. Check this out before you take action!) Sometimes it may not be cost-effective to open an estate in court to obtain ownership of smaller bank accounts, cars, etc. Even if the value of the property isn't much, it will drive your survivors crazy knowing that the property is there and they can't get to it!

Sounds great, right? Before you rush to put all your property into joint names, though, be aware of the possible downsides. Once you have transferred property into joint names, it may not be easy to undo if your relationship comes to an end. That can be a mess. Also, remember that by giving someone access to or an interest in your property, you are bearing the risk that that person might rip you off. This type of planning always involves an element of yielding control; do it with your eyes open.

Be extremely careful with all of your assets, assuming *nothing*. If you are entitled to any benefits through employment, etc., be *sure* to verify you have named a beneficiary for those benefits, *and* make sure they have the information on file. To make the pieces of your plan work together as a whole, you must understand the role played by each piece, and how they fit together.

Be especially careful that your plan as expressed through your will, and any death benefits to which you might be entitled, work together as a whole. Avoid such scenarios as the following:

> As an employee of the federal government, Dean is covered by an employee retirement plan to which he has contributed over the years. Since both Dean and his girlfriend, Sharon, are HIV-positive and have been ill, he strongly desires that Sharon inherit the funds in the plan after his death. He is especially concerned because he knows that his parents do not like Sharon and does not trust them to look after her if he dies.

Accordingly, Dean sees an attorney and has a will drawn up, leaving all of his estate to Sharon, and specifically stating his intention that none of his estate pass to his parents. A few months later, he dies, feeling that he has done everything within his power to protect Sharon.

Unfortunately, Sharon learns too late that under the rules of the retirement plan, those funds pass to family members (first spouse, then parents, etc.) *unless* the employee specifically documents *in forms provided by the plan administrators* a different beneficiary. Since Sharon is not a legal spouse, the employer does not care what the will says, and she is left destitute and out of luck.

Please don't let this happen to you and your loved ones. Any plan you have must work together as a whole, or not at all.

3

Are You Sure About How You Are Holding Title to Your Home?

For most people, their home is their greatest and most important asset. If you own a home or other real property, it is crucial that you know exactly how title to the property is held, and exactly what the consequences are. If you are legally married and hold title with your spouse on the deed (for example, if the two of you took title as "John Clark and Elizabeth Clark, Husband and Wife,") the two of you own the property as *tenants by the entireties,* and the property will automatically pass to your spouse if you die.

If you are not legally married, things can get more complicated. To start, there are two basic ways in which two unmarried people can hold title to property together:

1. **Joint tenants with rights of survivorship.** When A and B own property together in this form, full ownership of the property automatically vests in the survivor in the event one co-owner dies.
2. **Tenants in common.** When A and B do not specify "with rights of survivorship" *on the deed,* they are deemed to own the property in this form, regardless of their intention. If one of them dies, ownership does not automatically vest in the survivor. If, for instance, B dies, the property will automatically be owned one-half by A and one-half by the estate of B, so B's share will be distributed according to his will, or according to state law if B had had no will. Court involvement becomes

necessary in order to clear title to the property, requiring attorney involvement.

Time and again, I have had clients assume that they owned property with their life partners as joint tenants with survivorship rights, only to find out they were wrong. *Please,* if you own a home or any other real property with your life partner or anyone else, *take a look at your deed!* If you remember nothing else from this book, remember to do that. Please don't assume the deed says what you think it says; get it out and look at it! It is not enough for the deed to say *"A and B, as Joint Tenants."* If the deed does not contain the magic words *"with rights of survivorship,"* you've probably got a tenancy in common on your hands. Let's take a look at what that can mean:

> Eric and Brian invest their life savings in an oceanfront condominium, where they live together for several years. The condominium is in both their names. Although they believe that the property will pass to the survivor should one of them die, Eric suffers a rude awakening after Brian's untimely death. Because the deed contains no "rights of survivorship" language, Brian's one-half interest in the property passes to his estate. So now, instead of owning the condo outright, Eric finds himself sharing ownership with Brian's estate.

So what's the problem? Brian has left no will, thinking that "we don't have much besides the condo, and that would go to Eric." As a result, Brian's interest in the condominium automatically passes under the law to his homophobic and vindictive parents. Thus, in addition to dealing with the grief of his lover's loss, Eric now finds himself owning his home jointly with hostile strangers. To make matters worse, shortly thereafter, Brian's parents, who live in New Jersey, file papers in court trying to force a sale of the condo "so they can get their share." Unfortunately, as new co-owners of the property, they have a legal right to do so.

How's that for a nightmare scenario? But it can happen, and that is why it is so important to make sure that the language on your deed accurately expresses your intentions. The above example also illustrates the importance of having a complete and effective estate plan in place. Had Brian protected his lover by leaving a valid will in place, the property would have ended up in Eric's name with no hassle. (Even if the property had passed to Brian's estate, the will would have passed ownership back to Eric.) Beyond their other uses, wills make great safety nets. Even if you don't own much property now, you never know what your situation might be at the time you die.

Don't misunderstand; it is not necessarily bad to hold property as tenants in common if you have thought it through and that is what you want. Sometimes people choose to hold property that way to allow themselves to leave their interest in the property to their significant other, if they choose (through a will), or, if not, to anyone else they desire. Just be sure you understand what you're doing and make sure you're doing it right. Again, take a look at your deed. If the magic "survivorship" words are not there, and you want them to be, it is easy enough to redo the deed to reflect your true intentions. If that is the case, however, act now! And think seriously about using an attorney. This is important.

But before you leap please *do not* assume, without careful thought, that rights of survivorship are the right approach for you and your partner. If you want your share of the property to pass to anyone other than your partner, tenancy in common may be the way to go. Finally, if the two of you have a taxable estate (meaning $600,000 or more in assets), you must realize that you can be slammed with major estate-tax liabilities after one of you dies. If the property is held in joint tenancy with rights of survivorship, the full value of the home will be included in the estate of the first one of you to die, unless you can document, to the satisfaction of the IRS, the financial contribution each of you have made to the home. Then, after the death of the second partner, the full value of the property can be taxed once again. Ouch!

A couple of other potential problems exist with transferring title to your home. First, never forget that once title has been signed over, that cannot be undone without the consent of the new "joint owner." In the event of relationship problems, that can mean trouble. Also, if the person you're thinking of transferring title to is being pursued by creditors or has a history of poor credit, check with a local attorney before you take any action to make sure that you will not be putting your property at risk by transferring its ownership.

Once again: get some help in this area, it is important. Don't be taken by surprise!

4

What You Need to Know About Guardianship

In the preceding chapters, we have taken a look at some painful dramas that can unfold when people die without leaving wills, or when they die wrongly believing that their homes or other real property are held "with rights of survivorship" with their life partners or other chosen individuals. If you have HIV, a high likelihood exists that you are outside of the mainstream, and an extra burden falls upon you to protect yourself and those you love.

Although wills and trusts are extremely important, there is more to effective planning than simply planning for death. At some point in your life, you may need help with health care decisions or handling your finances. We'll now look at some of the problems that can hit people with HIV particularly hard, and the tools that are available to help stack the odds in their favor. Let's begin by taking a hard look at the possibility of incapacity, and exploring what can be done to avoid the painful battles that can erupt over guardianship.

GUARDIANSHIP IN A NUTSHELL

Whether or not you are HIV-positive, at some point in your life you may become incapacitated, meaning that you may need some help managing your life. While nobody likes to think about that possibility, much less have a plan in place just in case, it is crucial that you plan ahead.

Although battles fought over a will after someone's death can be highly charged, they cannot compare for sheer intensity or ugliness to a battle between a person's significant other and his or her family for control during that person's life. The effect can be devastating when people confronting either illness or injury become the center of a hard-fought controversy between the people in their lives. Consider the following scenario:

> Sean and Mark had been in a relationship for eight years when Sean became extremely ill with AIDS. Although throughout his adulthood Sean had chosen to have virtually no contact with his mother, a Christian fundamentalist who condemned his homosexuality, she began to visit Sean and Mark's home daily and to aggressively involve herself in her son's medical care as his condition worsened. Tension steadily grew between the mother and Mark, who found her intrusive and rudely dismissive of his relationship with Sean.
>
> As the arguments over Sean's medical care began to intensify, his mother began to accuse Mark of "letting my son die" so Mark could "inherit all of his property." Such allegations, made during an extremely stressful time in Mark's life, hit him hard. He developed such a paranoia that he became afraid to give his lover an aspirin for fear he would be attacked for it. Sean's mother had successfully driven a wedge between Sean and his caretaker.
>
> Finally, Sean's mother found a lawyer to file papers in court seeking her appointment as guardian "in order to save her son's life." After a court hearing, the court appointed an attorney to serve as temporary guardian instead of choosing either Sean's mother or Mark. Further, as required by the law, the court appointed an independent attorney to make sure Sean's interests were being represented in the guardianship proceeding.

At that point, Mark and Sean found themselves in the middle of an extremely intense and bizarre encounter with the legal system, surrounded by strangers (four of them lawyers) who had been given power over the most intimate decisions of their lives. Against Sean's will, the court gave his mother the right to visit him for one hour every day.

Finally, Sean, by that point very weak and in a wheelchair, was forced to defend himself in court proceedings. Although he was eventually found by the court not to be incapacitated, and the mother's suit was dismissed, the legal proceedings had ruined his last days, leaving him and his lover bitter. He died three weeks later.

Everyone with HIV should have a working plan for incapacity in place. Do not assume that the law will recognize your relationship, or your right to make health care or other decisions for one another unless you have taken specific action to make that happen.

If you or your loved one are ever forced to deal with incapacity, you will have enough problems on your hands without being forced to become players in a battle for control. That can happen if, for whatever reason, your family or your partner's choose to assert control over the situation. In such cases, having named your guardian in advance can forestall major hassles in court.

The only requirement to getting your situation in order is that you take an honest look at the possibilities and decide whom you would trust to handle your finances or make medical decisions for you if you became unable to do so. Think of it this way: you are not giving up control; you are actually taking charge of your life by reflecting on your needs as only you can and making the most difficult decisions for yourself, in advance. Why leave such important decisions up to others? Would you want your life decisions to be made by a judge who does not know you at all, and who may have an "issue" with who you are or the way you live? Decide for yourself.

The Solution: Naming Your Guardian in Advance

If you have made it this far without becoming totally depressed, congratulations: there is a light at the end of the tunnel! In many states, laws allow you to choose and name your guardian in advance by signing a document. Check out the laws of your state. Even if such documents are not specifically authorized, they may still serve as valuable evidence of your intention, which may carry great weight with the court in the unfortunate event that your situation comes down to a battle.

Naming a guardian in advance provides powerful protection; if you are ever found to need a guardian, the court is more likely to appoint the individual(s) you have named unless they are found to be unqualified to serve. Keep in mind that, without such a document or other appropriate documentation through a trust, blood relations will have priority of appointment over your life partner or whomever else you might want to name.

In chapter 1, we discussed the usefulness of trusts in planning for incapacity. By naming a successor trustee, and properly funding the trust, you have a working plan in place and should be able to avoid the need for a guardianship. Nevertheless, it is still a good idea to also name your guardian in advance. It cannot hurt to have your wishes well documented. In naming your guardian, be aware that you have a great range of choices in "custom tailoring" your situation to your needs. For example, you can name different people to serve as the "guardians of your *property*" (to handle your finances) and "guardians of your *person*" (to handle your medical care, housing, etc.). If the situation calls for it, you can also name coguardians to make joint decisions on your behalf. It is generally a good idea to keep it simple, but do not hesitate to create a plan that will work for you.

GUARDIANSHIP FOR CHILDREN

As HIV continues its sweep through American society, an increasing number of heterosexuals, many of them parents, are being forced to deal with the ravages of the disease. Many of these individuals are fairly young, too, including women of childbearing years, and are therefore taking care of young children. Further, many are single parents, with no backup available should the caretaker become ill or die. Obviously, one of the primary concerns of many parents in this situation is the well-being and long-term care of their children. What can be done to help meet that goal?

That is an important question because the worst possible course is to do nothing. If you fail to make any arrangements for the custody of your children, that task will fall to the state in the event of your death. Even if state workers are conscientious and mean well, they are generally overburdened and have no idea about the specific needs of your family and the children. Should the children become wards of the state, they may be separated from one another (especially if some of them are HIV-positive and some are not) and placed into foster homes or other facilities. Obviously, in the wake of having suffered your loss, such treatment can be completely disorienting to the children.

What can be done? A great deal, if proper planning is done and arrangements are put in place. Of all the tough issues presented by HIV, though, this is one of the toughest for people to face. The idea of leaving the children alone is terrifying for most parents; so much so that it seems easier not to think about the issue at all. While this "denial response" is easy to understand, it must be overcome for the benefit of the children.

What options in planning are available to you if you are a parent?

First, you can always state your wishes in your will. Additionally, the laws of some states specifically allow parents to name *preneed* or *standby* guardians for their children through separate documents. Just as you can name a guardian in advance for yourself, you can name one for your child. If two parents are involved, you should work on this question together, reach agreement if possible, and document your decision.

If you are a single parent, you may have more freedom to decide who would take care of the children in the event of your illness or death. In any event, of course, you need to make arrangements with the person you are naming. Never spring this on anyone by surprise; it is much too large a commitment and too important a decision. In fact, if possible, the ideal way to handle this transition is to allow the children to start spending time regularly with their prospective guardians, allowing a bond to start developing on both sides.

If two parents are involved in this decision and you can't agree, things can be a bit more complicated. Even if the other parent has never been involved in the child's life, he or she still has parental rights. Generally speaking, the surviving parent will be presumed by the court (if it comes down to a court battle) to be entitled to custody if you have died or become unable to care for the child. The court may find otherwise, however, if drug use, neglect, or other factors show that the surviving parent is not fit to handle the children.

If you are faced with such a situation, protecting your children will require more than simply signing a legal document. If you truly feel that placement with the children's other parent will be bad for them, you will need to request a hearing from the court to testify and to present evidence as to why you believe that to be the case. The court will evaluate whether the guardian you have chosen or the other parent would be the best guardian for the children and enter a court order to that effect.

A hassle? No question about it. Nevertheless, if it is important to you, you need to at least be aware of the possibility of pursuing such an action.

To sum it up: if you are HIV-positive and a parent of minor children, the ultimate act of love you can give them is to do your best to make arrangements for their care if anything happens to you. It will bring you at least some peace of mind, and that is important to both you and your child. You will have done everything you can do.

5

Using Powers of Attorney

As we've discussed in previous chapters, one of the most horrifying possibilities confronting people with HIV is the prospect of incapacity. Beyond the possibility of HIV brain involvement, or dementia, continued battles with various illnesses can take their toll, leaving one mentally and physically fatigued.

Unfortunately, life at that point often becomes more rather than less complicated, and important decisions need to be made. However, if you have done your best to put a plan in place, you and those you love will face less stress during that tough time and your lives may be made easier. In chapter 1, we discussed the use of trusts in planning for incapacity, and in chapter 4, the importance of having named a guardian in advance.

Now let's examine one of the most powerful tools available to help make sure that your finances don't fall apart if you become sick or otherwise disabled for a period of time: durable powers of attorney.

A **power of attorney** is a document by which one person grants authority to another to take specific actions on his or her behalf.

Any person (called the principal) can delegate as much or as little power as desired to any other person, who is then authorized to act as the principal's agent. The documents can grant specific and limited authority, such as the right to sell a car or a home, can be limited to a particular time ("I authorize Rupert to manage my finances and to run my business until September 1"), or can be unlimited in scope or duration. With that kind of flexibility, you can imagine how useful the documents can be in planning for incapacity.

Until recently, however, there was a serious problem in that context: *the documents became invalid, and therefore useless, as soon as the principal became incapacitated.*

In many states, that is no longer the case. You can now name any person, family or not, to act for you in the event you become disabled. With the advent of durable powers, an important new door has opened for disability planning. The laws of many states now specifically allow you to name anyone to act for you in any necessary way, and that delegation will remain valid even if you become injured or too sick to handle your own affairs. I can hear you thinking "So what?" Consider the following simple scenarios:

> Gilberto, who is HIV-positive, owns a small apartment building. He alone collects the rents, pays the bills, including the mortgage, and maintains the property. What might happen in the event of his sickness?
>
> Jill's sole source of income now is her disability payments, from which she pays her rent, buys her groceries, etc. Who will cash her checks and pay her bills and feed her pets if she is hospitalized?

The examples go on and on in an infinite variety of possibilities. Although nobody likes to think about the possibility of being incapacitated, much less planning for it, it is crucial for you to take a look at your situation and to foresee what your needs might be if you became unable to run your own show for a while, and to make your best judgment call on who you think would be the right person (that means able *and* willing), if any, to take on that commitment for you. The plan that is right for you may involve a durable power of attorney.

Once again, it is not too hard to put a plan in place—if you are willing to plan ahead. Why is that so important? Previously, we have discussed the true horror stories and ugly power struggles that can result from battles over guardianship. The good news, though, is that the entire guardianship process can be avoided if a person has put in place a plan in advance. One important part of that plan can be a durable power.

An important note: Even though durable powers remain valid even after the principal has become incapacitated, they *do not* remain in effect after the principal has died. Once the bank learns that the principal has died, they will no longer honor the power of attorney. Further, even if you succeed in having the bank release the funds to you before it learns of the death, you may find yourself in trouble if family members or others learn you have "illegally" used the power of attorney to access funds when you either knew or should have known that the document was no longer valid. Keep your eyes open on this one!

For all their powerful advantages, durable powers can also mean big trouble. The very qualities that can make them so useful also make them potentially dangerous. The main advantage of a durable power is that the person you choose can handle your affairs, including your finances, without supervision even if you become incapacitated. Which is great, unless the person you have named is dishonest and rips you off.

That has happened. In some cases, people with AIDS have come home from the hospital only to find their lovers gone and their bank accounts cleaned out through the use of powers of attorney. Their lovers, reasoning that their partners were so sick they probably weren't coming out of the hospital anyway, had anticipated ugly battles with their partner's families in the probate courts or had just gotten tired and simply left. Although no one likes to think that he or his partner would be capable of such action, the stress, fear, and grief involved in that kind of situation can probably not be imagined until you are in it.

So how can you protect yourself from abuses?

First, do not rush and name just anyone as your agent through a power of attorney without a great deal of thought. Get good legal advice. Numerous planning possibilities exist for you based upon your individual situation. You might want to name two people you trust to act for you jointly, or delegate only narrow powers to your agent, or name one person to handle your finances and another to make your medical decisions. Think about whether a trust, or even some simple planning with joint bank accounts (chapter 6), might take care of your particular needs.

Second, remember that durable powers often become effective as soon as they are signed, unless you indicate a contrary intention within the document. (The laws of some states allow for "springing" powers, becoming effective only upon the occurrence of certain contingencies.) The practical problem, however, is that such clauses make banks or other financial institutions extremely nervous and less likely to rely on the documents. As a practical alternative, arrangements can be made to keep the documents in safe hands until they are needed. Here's an example:

> Kenny signs a durable power naming his lover, Tom, as his agent to act on Kenny's behalf in the event he becomes incapacitated. He signs a letter requesting that his attorney not release the document to Tom until Kenny's doctor, his attorney, and Tom agree that Kenny has become incapacitated to the point where he needs assistance managing his affairs. The document will therefore not be released unless it is ever needed.

Despite their dangers, durable powers can be a valuable part of an effective personal plan in certain cases. Get help and legal advice, though; don't try to walk this one alone. Further, if you do decide to make a durable power part of your overall plan, do not automatically assume that banks, brokerage houses, etc., will honor the documents. It is a good idea to submit the signed power of attorney to the bank or other financial institution involved, and to confirm with them that it will be honored. It's probably an even better idea to request and complete one of the bank's own power of attorney forms. Banks are extremely fearful of liability in this area and generally feel much more comfortable with their own forms.

If you ever become incapacitated and the power of attorney is really needed, it will be too late to start hassling with the bank to protect your wishes. Don't let this vital link in your chain of disability planning let you down.

Finally, it is important to realize that *you can change your mind at any time,* even if you have already signed your documents. A power, durable or otherwise, only lasts as long as you want it to. If you do choose to revoke your documents, though, do it right. Make sure that every person, bank, or other relevant financial institution that has gotten a copy knows that the document is no longer any good. Seek an attorney's help in making sure that your revocation will be complete and effective. You do not want a durable power to remain in the wrong hands.

6

You and Your Bank Accounts

We are now going to tell you how to get more bang for your planning buck, so listen up!

No matter what the details of your personal or financial situation might be, if you have any money in the bank at all, you will find information in this section that you can use to simply and effectively plan for the future and protect your loved ones.

We will now take a look at the range of planning available to you using your bank accounts, brokerage accounts, or most other accounts containing financial investments. Let's focus on the areas of concern most important to people with HIV: **estate planning** and **planning for incapacity**.

Consider the following examples:

> After Norma Jean becomes seriously ill, she is no longer able to write checks or to endorse for deposit any incoming checks. As a result, her boyfriend faces mounting financial pressure as he receives a preliminary notice of foreclosure from the bank and starts being hassled by other creditors. He does not know what to do.
>
> Victor is killed in a car accident, never having made out a will. Because his longtime lover, Jon, has had ongoing credit problems for years and anticipated being sued, he had sheltered some of his assets in a bank account held in

Victor's name alone. After Victor's death, Jon is unable to access any funds from the account. Victor's family proceeds to open up an estate to obtain the $40,000 held in the account, and Jon is probably out of luck.

Eddie dies, having conscientiously made out a will leaving his largest asset, an account containing almost $100,000, to Ginger, his secret paramour of ten years. Unfortunately, Eddie is underinsured and hospitalized for several months. By the time he dies, his medical debts far exceed the amount of his estate. After creditors file claims and take their share of the estate, nothing is left for Ginger.

Quick: before we sink any further into total depression, let's take a look at some possibilities in creative banking to help avoid scenarios such as the above. Think about the following possibilities.

Often, lovers or other people whose finances might be commingled keep their funds in "joint accounts." If your account is jointly titled in the names of "A *or* B," then *either* A or B will be able to withdraw funds from the account. That can be great in terms of giving yourself a little flexibility in case you, for whatever reason, ever need a little help in handling your financial affairs. Further, if the account is titled this way at the time of your death, the co-owner who survives you will automatically be entitled to inherit whatever remains in the account, directly and without going through probate. (State law on this point may vary, so be sure to confirm this with your bank if it is important to you.) That means that, unless unusual circumstances exist, creditors probably won't get a good shot at the money after your death.

But, beware of the possible downside! First, once the other person's name is on the account, he or she will be legally authorized to withdraw all of the funds from the account. You may therefore have to ask yourself some hard questions prior to changing the title to your accounts. How much do you really trust your life partner, friend, or whomever you're thinking of? Could he or she be tempted to split with the money? How might the person react under stress?

If disagreements later arise between you and the other person, or the other person wrongfully withdraws funds, he or she may claim that you had made a gift of the funds, or that he or she had contributed to the account. Even if those statements are not true, they can create a lot of smoke if you are forced to seek return of the money through court proceedings.

Second, depending on the financial status of the other person, you should be aware that his or her creditors (including possibly the bank!) may try to claim part or all of the account on the basis, true or not, that the account belongs to the other person. Don't feel that you need plan on an "all or nothing" basis. In other words, think about putting only *part* of your money, however much may be necessary, in joint names. Think carefully about the plan that may be right for you, and be creative.

ITF OR POD ACCOUNTS

You also need to *definitely* understand and be aware of how ITF (in trust for) accounts work. In some states, these accounts are referred to as POD (payable on death) accounts. Practically speaking, the concepts are the same. If you have titled your account(s) this way, your chosen beneficiary will automatically be entitled to receive the funds after your death.

> If Maria and Jerry have an account titled "Maria ITF Jerry," the funds unquestionably belong to Maria alone during her lifetime. If she chooses to spend part or all of the money during her lifetime, she can, and Jerry will have nothing to say about it. However, any money left in the account at the time of Maria's death will automatically pass to Jerry. All Jerry need do to obtain the funds at that point would be to

> visit the bank with a copy of Maria's death certificate, and the bank would release them to him. Further, none of Maria's creditors will ordinarily be able to get to the money. If Jerry died before Maria, she could simply change her named beneficiary.

The beauty of these accounts, again, is that you and only you have *complete* control of the funds during your lifetime. If you change your mind at any time, you can simply withdraw the funds or retitle the account. After your death, however, your chosen beneficiary will be protected. Had either Victor or Eddie in the examples above designated the accounts in question as ITF or POD for their chosen beneficiaries, those scenarios would have had happier endings.

DIRECT DEPOSIT OF PAYCHECKS/BENEFITS

Often, people encounter major problems with getting access to their money when they become seriously ill.

They may not be able to endorse their checks or to get to the bank. Often, people receiving social security benefits, or living on disability payments, run into problems when they are hospitalized or otherwise become too sick to cash their checks. Landlords who are eager to dump their disabled tenants have sometimes moved quickly to evict them when rent remains unpaid, and other major hassles can result from having some money but not being able to get to it.

A good simple way to minimize this problem?

Try direct deposit. The benefits can be transferred automatically into your account every month, and you can allow a trusted person access to that account to help make sure that your bills are paid, etc., in the event you become unable to handle it for a while.

> For example, Mark requests that his social security payments be direct-deposited into an account that he has titled

> jointly in the names of "Mark or Laura." That way, his friend Laura is able to get to the funds and pay Mark's bills when he has to be hospitalized for an extended period.
>
> Alternatively, if Laura has her own problems and is at risk for hassles from creditors, Mark can simply authorize her to be a "signatory" on the account instead of formally adding her name to the account. Either way, she can get to the money if necessary.

Remember, though, that the person holding your account jointly can withdraw all of the funds if he or she chooses to. If you feel insecure, just appropriately limit the amount of money kept in the account.

As another possibility, at least with regard to his social security check, Mark can fill out a form with the Social Security Administration naming Laura as his *representative payee,* and she will be authorized to legally receive his check for him. (We'll discuss social security issues in chapter 12.)

Also think about the feasability of arranging for automatic payment of your bills. Some banks offer such a service, ensuring that your mortgage, utilities, and other important bills will not go unpaid. Alternatively, you can ask someone you trust to help see to it that those payments are made. That way, even if you are sick or otherwise thrown for a loop for a couple of months, at least your home and related expenses will be secure.

7

Planning for Your Health Care Needs: Naming Your Health Care Proxy

Let's now focus on another important arena of planning, health care decision making, and begin with a look at one of the most simple, powerful, and effective tools available to you in planning ahead.

By signing a simple document, which in your state may be called a health care "proxy" or "surrogate," you can name any individual you want to make health care decisions for you in the event you became unable to make them for yourself. That you may be in a relationship with your named surrogate is irrelevant. All the hospitals or other health care providers need know or care about is that you have chosen that person to act as your agent for health care purposes.

Never before has it been so easy to protect yourself in such an important way. Not only are the documents accepted by hospitals, doctors, and other health care providers, they are strongly encouraged. Look at the situation from their point of view: the last thing hospitals want is to find themselves embroiled in a conflict between a patient's blood relations and his or her significant other because those parties disagree on the appropriate medical procedure to follow, or to be unable to proceed with necessary medical treatment because the patient is unable to consent and no "family members" are available to give a green light. Under such circumstances, the hospital is damned if it does and if it doesn't.

In addition to consenting to medical treatment and accepting or rejecting proposed medical procedures, your surrogate can also be given authority to review your medical records, check you in and out of hospitals, and apply for public benefits on your behalf. In short, the document empowers your chosen representative to stand in your shoes for all medical purposes. It is important that you choose someone you're comfortable with, and who knows you well.

The documents have become increasingly common and popular, not only because they are so useful, but because hospitals, nursing homes, etc., are now required by federal law, under the Patient's Self-Determination Act, to inform their patients of their state's law with respect to their right to name a surrogate, and to make a *living will* stating their wishes as to artificial life support. (We will tackle that one in the next chapter.) There is no good reason anyone should not name a surrogate in advance. Avoid such scenarios as the following:

> When Quentin suffers an adverse reaction to HIV medication and loses consciousness, his lover, Oscar, rushes him to the emergency room at the nearest hospital. After Quentin is admitted to the hospital, the hospital refuses to provide any information whatsoever to Oscar about his lover's whereabouts, his treatment, or his medical condition. Despite Oscar's shock, grief, and mounting frustration, hospital officials explain to him that gay lovers are not recognized as "family" under hospital policy, and that therefore the hospital could suffer liability if it discloses information on Quentin's medical condition without his consent to Oscar.

Even worse and more tragic abuses have occurred:

> Archie and Mehitabel had lived together in Hollywood for over ten years when Archie is hospitalized with a serious AIDS diagnosis. When his parents are notified, they move to L.A. to "make sure our son is taken care of." Much of their rage at their son's suffering becomes directed at "that tramp," Mehitabel, "who probably gave Archie the damn

virus in the first place." The family gives strict instructions to the hospital that absolutely no information on Archie's treatment or medical condition is to be released to Mehitabel and directs that visits to Archie are to be limited to "family members." With Archie too sick to object, and Mehitabel too deeply in shock and unaware of her rights to force the issue, the family succeeds in building an invisible wall between the two.

By the time Mehitabel learns from a friend that her partner of ten years has died, Archie has been dead for over a week, he has been buried, and the family has already held his funeral and returned home.

How could the above scenario have been different? Had Archie signed a document naming Mehitabel his "health care proxy," she would have had clear legal priority over the family when the conflict arose over Archie's medical care. Further, had Archie named Mehitabel in his living will as his agent for purposes of pulling the plug, (chapter 8) she would probably have at least received notice of her partner's passing.

So we return to the ongoing theme: *do not expect the law to do it for you; protect yourself.* The legal hassles that can result from conflict over this issue, on top of illness, can be devastating. The good news: unlike certain other important documents, which should always be done with the advice of an attorney, you *do not* need an attorney to sign these documents. Ask your doctor or a local hospital for the forms and fill them out! You will be glad you did.

Again, don't be afraid that by naming a health care surrogate you are giving up power over your life. First, if you break up with your life partner or otherwise change your mind, you can always change your named surrogate. (If that happens, simply do your best to replace all known copies, in your medical records and elsewhere, with your new document, and let the appropriate people know.) Second, as long as you remain able to make your own medical decisions, you have full right to do so. Even if, for example, you choose to reject all medical treatment, that is your right. Unless unusual circumstances exist (e.g., you are a pregnant woman), you are subject to virtually no restrictions, so long as you are able to understand the decision you are making and its consequences. Similarly, it is not too late to name a health care surrogate even if you have been sick, so long as you have the present mental ability to do so. No matter what your health situation, do it now.

Note: Please realize that the signed document will do you no good if it is not available when and where you need it. Accordingly, after you have signed the document, make sure to give a copy to your doctor (if you have one) for your medical file, and also make sure that your named surrogate has a copy. If you are admitted to the hospital, make sure that your surrogate has been told to make a copy of the document (and also your living will, which we will discuss in the next chapter) and have it placed in your hospital file.

When does the document legally take effect? It will kick in only when you have lost the ability to make your own medical decisions, and when your physician has documented that in your file. The documents can be a vital safety net that can protect your wishes when you need that protection most. Don't let this one slide!

8

Thinking About Your Living Will

Never before have people facing the prospect of incapacity had at their disposal a wider and more effective variety of tools to take control over their futures, including their health care, than are now available. Largely as a result of lobbying by advocates for the disabled, including those affected by HIV, the laws of many states now recognize the rights of their citizens to make the difficult medical decisions for themselves, and to safeguard those wishes by signing legally enforceable documents. One of the most important of those documents is a living will.

A **living will** is the document by which you can state your wish to be allowed to die, and not to be kept alive by "artificial means," if you are ever in a terminal condition and are probably not coming out of it.

Why do so many people feel so strongly that the documents are important? There are a number of reasons.

First, as a constructive response to the challenges of living with HIV, we have learned to take an active role in our medical treatment. We have learned to weigh risks and benefits in proposed procedures, and to sometimes reject treatments if the pain or possible risks overshadow the possible benefit. Unfortunately, when death is near, people are often unable to make their own decisions. Yet what medical decision is more important than the ultimate decision that "enough is enough, let's stop the suffering and let the patient go"?

The only way you can effectively make this crucial decision known is through a living will.

Second, the documents are crucial because many doctors, hospitals, and other health providers strongly resist allowing patients in their care to die. This resistance is based on several factors: their often unquestioned idea that life must be preserved at any cost, their fears of malpractice and liability, and seen cynically, the fact that money is to be made from providing medical services on an ongoing basis.

Advocates of the documents see them as essential to help patients avoid being caught in a twilight-zone web of medical technology long after all quality of life life is gone, while their opponents see them as yet another dangerous step on the slippery slope to sanctioning suicide. Court decisions, best-selling literature, and the vigorous debate on our "right to die" all reflect our society's ongoing fascination with this issue. If the dispute can be seen as a nationwide debate, the "right to die" side is winning; it is clear that people are no longer willing to yield control on their right to make that ultimate decision.

What are your options in making a living will? Plenty. First, you have the right to document your desire not to be kept alive by artificial means if you are ever in a terminal condition and not likely to improve, as confirmed by the opinion of an independent physician. In some states, the term *terminal condition* is defined as including a permanent vegetative state, raising the possibility that "artificial means" in that context might include feeding through tubes or hydration (IV administration of fluids).

The field is open for you to dictate, as specifically as you wish, whatever treatment (or lack thereof) you would desire if you were ever in that position. In many states, also, you are specifically authorized to name the person you would choose to make the decision to withdraw further treatment on your behalf. Once again, if you fail to specify otherwise, that right will probably pass to blood relations.

It is important to distinguish this agent from your health care surrogate: although they can be the same person, their roles are different. The agent named in your living will becomes involved only if you are near death and a decision needs to be made about withholding further medical treatment or sustenance. Your health care surrogate, in contrast, becomes involved as soon as you become even temporarily unable to make your own health care decisions. For full protection, you need both documents in place.

Even though it is not easy, in taking the time to think about these questions, you are doing a great favor to your life partner, family, or other loved ones. Don't leave them, in a time of grief, to make the mind-blowing decision of whether your time has come. The only way you, and they, can be sure that your wishes will be understood and followed is for you to make decisions in advance.

In this area, laws can differ significantly from state to state. To get important information on the specifics of your state's law, call the helpful staff at Choice in Dying, Inc., an organization based in Newark, New Jersey, dedicated to education and advocacy regarding peoples' right to choose on issues relating to health care in the terminal stages. See appendix B.

"Do Not Resuscitate" (DNR) Orders

You should also be aware that some states specifically authorize the signing of "DNR" Orders, by which you request that you not be given cardio-pulmonary resuscitation in the event of coronary failure. Be aware that, unless these specific documents are signed, emergency rescue personnel will be legally required to use heroic measures to "bring you back," even though you are suffering, are very near death, or would not have wanted such measures to be administered to you.

If this is of concern to you, please discuss it with your caretaker and your physician, and make your wishes clearly known in a way the law will recognize. In this area, above all others, strict compliance with the letter of the law is key. Please understand that emergency rescue personnel are acting under extreme pressure (as well as heavy fears of legal liability), and your wishes will *not* be recognized unless you have fully complied with the requirements of the law in terms of the form of the document, etc. Recognize that in some states, unlike the Health Care Proxy and the Living Will, these documents must be prepared anew prior to each hospital admission in order to remain effective. If this is important to you, please do your best to get it right.

9

Navigating the Quicksands: How to Safeguard Your Documents Against Attack

As we have been exploring, people outside the mainstream too often encounter a rude awakening upon being dragged into a legal system that does not necessarily recognize the validity of their relationships. Tragic injustice often results when people die without having provided for their life partners or others close to them through a will or other plan. Too often, the survivors left behind learn the hard way, when it is too late, that the law will not recognize their rights.

In previous chapters, we have explored some of the other crucial documents available to you as "pieces of the puzzle" in putting together a comprehensive plan that is right for you. As we've discussed, the absence of legally effective documents can make or break your situation. If you have failed to protect yourself, painful battles can result.

Because these documents are so crucial, it is important to understand the basic grounds on which they are often attacked, and to protect yourself against these attacks to the extent possible. Although an "airtight" document cannot be guaranteed, certain precautions can greatly help. Remember, too, that even if the documents do not prevent litigation, they make it much more likely that justice will prevail if it becomes necessary to argue the issue in court.

If we lived in a more accepting society, and if the stakes were not so high, we might have a greater margin for error, but we don't. So here we go.

ATTACK #1: UNDUE INFLUENCE

Probably the most common attack on these documents, and especially wills, is a claim of "undue influence." In making that claim, the person attacking the document argues that the document does not reflect the true intention of the person who has signed it, but instead has been "procured" by someone else. If that claim is proven, the document is found invalid and treated as if it didn't exist. Consider the following examples:

> After David dies, leaving a will naming his lover, Ben, as the beneficiary of his entire estate, David's family files a lawsuit claiming that the will is invalid as a product of "undue influence." Believing that "there's no way our son would have cut us out of his will," the family argues that Ben orchestrated the preparation and signing of the will by driving David to the office of Ben's attorney to sign the will shortly after David had gotten out of the hospital. Ben is forced to defend himself in painful court proceedings, and no one can be sure of the outcome.
>
> In order to obtain life insurance coverage, Jose had named his mother as the intended beneficiary of the policy. According to his plan, he later signed and mailed in the change of beneficiary form naming his life partner, Michael. After Jose's death, his mother filed a lawsuit seeking the proceeds of the policy, arguing that Michael must have applied "undue influence" to Jose to persuade him to name him as a beneficiary. Lengthy litigation ensues.

The examples go on and on. Gay people and others outside the mainstream must be extremely cautious in foreseeing this claim because, when it is raised, the relationship itself is often put on trial. Any weaknesses in either individual in the relationship, or in the relationship itself, are bound to become issues in the court. Unfortunately, too, many courts seem predisposed to recognize the rights of a parent or sibling over partners in nontraditional relationships. Many judges just don't get it.

To further complicate matters, many courts evaluating claims of undue influence have ruled that ill people, needing assistance to meet their daily needs, are especially vulnerable to inappropriate influence. Further, courts have sometimes upheld such attacks on the grounds that the beneficiary under the challenged document was a caretaker to the ill person, placing them in an ideal position to unduly influence.

What can be done about such obnoxious claims? Obviously, if your significant other is ill, you must be a caretaker and there is nothing to be done about that. The key, then, becomes to consciously create a record that any will or other document that is being signed by your partner reflects his or her true wishes, and not yours.

How can you do that? If you are in a committed relationship, the key is to go to whatever lengths necessary to avoid even the appearance that you are "procuring" the document from your life partner. If the red flags of family hostility are present, think about using separate attorneys to document your estate plans. In short, use whatever creative means may be necessary to create a record that the document reflects the true wishes of the person signing it. Some of the safeguarding techniques mentioned in the next section should be of assistance to you in this task.

ATTACK #2: LACK OF MENTAL CAPACITY

As obnoxious as this claim is, it seems to be growing in popularity as HIV continues its awful spread. If it can be shown that a person lacked mental capacity at the time he or she executed the documents, they are invalid and of no legal effect. If you are HIV-positive, even if you are feeling completely healthy, some simple steps should be taken to help avoid this claim.

Too often, after people die of AIDS, their documents are attacked on the basis that "they must have been infected when they did the documents, and they didn't know what they were doing." Although the claim is often meritless, expert testimony as to AIDS dementia, or the mental fatigue resulting from prolonged battles with sickness, can be damaging and lead to stressful court battles.

Do not misunderstand: no matter how sick you are or may have been, you do have the legal right to sign these documents. Even if someone has suffered from long-term dementia, it may be possible to uphold the documents in court if they are found to be signed during a "lucid interval," when the person had clarity of mind and understood what he or she was doing. You just need to be careful, again, in creating a record that mental capacity is not truly an issue.

How can that be done? Consider the following possibilities:

- One of the most simple and effective means to document your mental capacity is to ask for your doctor's help. Try to schedule a doctor's appointment as close as possible, if not on the same day, to the time you plan to sign your documents. Ask your doctor to make a note in your medical records as to your capacity. In most states, to be able to make a will you need only understand the general nature of your property, whom you are leaving it to, and that that is the purpose of the will. So long as you understand those elements, the will should be upheld, even if you are ultimately found to have been mentally impaired to some degree.

    As to any other documents, you need only understand their purpose and want to sign them. If you anticipate a challenge from hostile relatives, ask your doctor to be as detailed as possible in the notations. If your documents are ever challenged,

those notes could be extremely helpful to you and your loved ones if they are forced to protect themselves in court.
- It may be helpful to take the time to write out, in your own handwriting, your wishes. That should show both that the documents reflect your wishes as opposed to your partner's or anyone else's (undue influence), and that you knew what you were doing.
- Finally, you may want to consider videotaping the signing of the documents, as well as an interview of your feelings on these issues. If you look good, a videotape can be great evidence. On the other hand, physical weakness can sometimes create an impression of mental disability, even if that is not really the case. This strategy needs to be evaluated on a case-by-case basis. If you feel that videotaping may not be a good idea, think about having a court reporter attend an "interview" and signing of the documents, so that at least your words can be preserved. Be sure to identify your family members in specific detail, and explain your exact motivations and reasons for making disposition as you have chosen to do.

  In order to avoid an appearance of undue influence, your life partner should not be involved in any aspect of this process, and should probably not even be shown the tape while you are alive.
- Choose your witnesses carefully. If you anticipate a hassle, it might be worth it to have a person trained in mental health issues attend and witness your will signing. Alternatively, if possible it might be wise to have respected and objective members of your community, such as members of the clergy, etc., witness your documents if you fear they might be attacked.

In Summary

Other attacks are also commonly raised, such as fraud, forgery, and coercion. But don't lose heart; these claims are extremely difficult to prove without a factual basis. Remember, you do have the right to express your wishes in these documents and to have them be given legal effect and followed. To make that happen, though, you may have to be aware and actively protect yourself against these attacks. It can be done, but you have got to follow through.

10

Introduction to Insurance Issues: Covering the Basics

No assets are more important to people living with HIV than good health, life, and disability insurance coverage, yet few subjects can be as intimidating. If the very idea of insurance stirs in you feelings of helplessness and despair, you are not alone. After all, the insurance companies have written your policies, defined terms as they see fit, and in short set up the rules of the serious game in which you are forced to play. In approaching any insurance issue or dispute, therefore, it may be wise to recognize from the start that, to a certain extent, you will be playing the game on their turf. To prevail, you will literally need to beat them at their own game.

That does not mean that you cannot win a dispute with an insurance company, or that you are powerless to push your insurer to provide you with a higher level of service. It simply means that, to achieve your desired result on any insurance issue, you must take the time to research and fully understand the contents of your policy *before* you act.

Also, be extremely careful as you deal with insurance companies. Try to develop a polite relationship with claims managers or others whom you deal with in your insurance company, but always keep in mind that the situation could quickly become adversarial. Accordingly, you should keep a journal outlining the specifics of each conversation with your insurance company, and open a file to save *all* correspondence, billing information, or other documentation received by you from the company. Otherwise, such information may "disappear" if it would help your position.

Here's the ideal balance: do not necessarily *expect* problems with your insurer, but be neither surprised nor unprepared if they arise.

Stripped to its basics, insurance law is nothing more or less than a matter of contract, in which the insurer agrees to assume on your behalf certain specifically defined obligations, under specifically defined conditions, so long as you do your part under the contract (i.e., refrain from fraud and keep paying your premiums). It is that simple, and that complicated!

The more complete your understanding of the important provisions of your coverage, the more possible it will be for you either to avoid problems in the first place or to resolve them with a minimum of stress and acrimony if they do arise. If you are currently employed, it is crucial that you immediately research your benefits. Are you currently covered by health, life, and/or disability insurance through your employer? Have you reviewed a copy of your employee benefits handbook and evaluated the specifics of each type of coverage? Before you go any further in this chapter, get in hand copies of any such policies currently in force. Although it can be challenging, do your best to try and read through and understand how the policies work, and how they will work in your situation.

If you do not have a copy of any such policies, get one. (Summaries of benefits offer a good start, and do not hesitate to request them, but the better practice is to turn to the policy itself.) If you are covered as an individual, request a replacement copy of your policy either through your insurance agent or directly from the insurance company. If you are covered as part of a group (most typically through employment), things can get a little more difficult. First, ask your employer for copies of any insurance documents covering you. If they have a copy and for any reason resist providing it to you, politely but firmly insist upon your rights. Sometimes, however, depending on the size of the group and its relationship with the insurer, your employer may not have a copy of the "master policy" covering the group, and it may be difficult even for them to obtain one. Further, in many cases the language of the master policy can be clouded by amendments and revisions, making it a real challenge to decipher your rights under the policy.

If all else fails, and you are unable to get answers to the questions important to you, the best strategy may be for you to submit to your employer, or its benefits department, carefully written questions designed to elicit the information you need, and to ask that the questions be answered by someone with authority to do so.

Even after you have your policies in hand and sit down to read them, however, you may find yourself confronted by complicated language and legal terms that mean nothing to you. You may be tempted to throw up your hands in despair and give up. Please do not! Your coverage is too important to you. First, grab a dictionary and sit down to read the *definitions section* in your policy. If that does not help to clear up your confusion, ask anyone who you think might be able to help you for an opinion, such as your insurance agent (or one referred to you by a local AIDS services organization or the AIDS hot line in your state), a case manager, or an attorney.

If you give up on trying to understand your rights or the insurer's obligations as set forth in your policy, you are yielding to the insurer a great deal of control, and trusting that they will act in accordance with your best interests. That can be extremely dangerous. The way the system is set up, it is *your* role and not the insurer's to make sure that you are receiving the level of coverage to which you are entitled. Don't even think about giving up that power. It may be their policy, but this is *your* life.

Do not be afraid to ask your employer questions about any of your benefits. Under ordinary circumstances, doing so should *not* necessarily serve as a "red flag" triggering their curiosity about your HIV status. After all, most employees, no matter what the status of their health, either are or should be concerned about the quality of their coverage. If any questions arise, simply tell them that you just want to know. Alternatively, explain to them that you are thinking about consulting with a lawyer for an estate plan, and that you need the information for that purpose. Your motivations are none of their business.

It is important to understand that any health, life, or disability coverage you have in force can literally become a lifeline. If you remember nothing else from this chapter, *please* remember to see to it that those premiums get paid. Especially after you have left your job, the burden falls on you alone to make sure that your coverage is kept in force. Too often, the serious financial pressure following illness leads people to stop paying premiums, and lapse of coverage is a huge problem in the HIV community. If you let that happen, rest assured that the insurance company will not shed a tear.

At a minimum, carefully note and calendar all due dates and grace periods for your insurance coverage. If possible, set up your finances (chapters 5 and 6) so that someone you trust will be able to make payments for you, through a power of attorney or other banking arrangement, if you are hospitalized or otherwise cannot. If you can afford it, pay up your premiums annually or semiannually to minimize the possibility of lapse. Alternatively, think about setting up recurring premium payments through direct transfers from your bank.

Finally, state assistance may be available through the federal Ryan White Act or otherwise to help pay your health insurance premiums even if you are not completely indigent. However, some financial limitations may apply. Call *immediately* an AIDS services organization near you or your state AIDS hot line or your state's health department to get more information.

If keeping *life insurance* coverage in force is your concern, no state assistance may be available. If that is the case, be creative and try to work out a deal with family and/or friends. In return for funds loaned to keep the coverage in force, arrange to repay them, with interest, either after your death or after you have viaticated the policy. Use your imagination and structure a deal that works for you.

SOME IMPORTANT DEFINITIONS

At best, this chapter of the book is intended to give you only general guidance through the thicket of insurance law. Please remember that insurance coverage is nothing more or less than a matter of contract, completely defined and governed by the terms of your policy. The resolution of virtually any insurance question, therefore, *must* start with a careful reading of the terms of your policy. Do not assume that your policy says what you would like it to; read it through!

Let's look at a few of the more important definitions with which you should be familiar and explore what they might mean to you.

- **Incontestability clause.** Most common in life and disability insurance policies, such provisions limit an insurer's ability to challenge the validity of the policy for any reason (except the nonpayment of premiums) after it has been in force for a certain time, usually two years. Such provisions are required under the law of many states. Generally speaking, even if erroneous statements were made in your application, or if relevant information was omitted, the policy should be honored if it has been in force for the required period.

  If you have passed the incontestability period but good-faith grounds might exist for the insurer to attack the coverage, are you home free? That's what the language would appear to indicate, but that may not necessarily be the case. From the beginning of the epidemic, insurance companies have struggled with the problem of fitting HIV, an entirely new and different phenomenon, into the existing framework of insurance law to keep on doing "business as usual." Never before had such a devastating illness with such an extended latency period reared its ugly head, and insurers have desperately begun to try to carve exceptions into incontestability provisions.

In some states, insurers have successfully argued that fraud overrides an incontestability provision, and in others the provisions have been upheld. Although such provisions are generally still given full force and effect, you might want to check out any court decisions in your state if you have reason for concern.

This issue ties into our next definition.

- **Rescission.** The law generally permits an insurer to elect to void the contract and simply return any premiums it has collected, if you have made a *material misrepresentation* that has induced them to issue the coverage to you when they otherwise would not have. Although the result may feel the same to you, rescission is not the same as cancellation. Unlike cancellation, which acknowledges that a policy was in force, rescission treats the matter as if the insurance contract had never existed. All you have left to show for the experience is a refund of any premiums you may have paid.

  What is a *material misrepresentation*? Good question. This is a legal concept fluid in its meaning and dependent on the facts and circumstances of each case. Generally, a misrepresentation is *material* (loosely translated as "really important") if the insurer can prove that it would not have extended the coverage to you had it known the truth. The more eager an insurer is to dump your coverage, the more closely they are likely to scrutinize your application and your medical history, and to define any errors in the application as *material*, even if they are honest and trivial mistakes.

  If you ever receive notice of rescission from your insurer, consult an attorney. *Do not* cash the check they may have sent you representing a refund of your premiums; your doing so might be interpreted as a concession to their point of view.

  A possible defense can be raised if the insurer did not rescind your policy in strict accordance with its underwriting guidelines. For example, if they *really* dumped you because of HIV, but *said* they were dumping you because of your alleged failure to disclose some insignificant medical condition or past treatment, you can carefully examine the insurer's underwriting guidelines to determine whether they failed to follow their own rules in voiding your coverage. This area of the law can get extremely technical, and professional advice is recommended.

- **Preexisting condition exclusions.** Typically, health and disability insurers seek to limit their liability by excluding from coverage, sometimes outright and sometimes for a period of time, payment for treatment of an insured's medical condition that existed before or at the time the person became covered.

  A couple of interesting definitional questions arise concerning HIV as a preexisting condition. First, does having asymptomatic HIV, by itself, necessarily mean that you have a "preexisting condition" in terms of obtaining new coverage? It should not. Look at the policy definitions: if "sickness" or "illness" is required, or the illness is required to have become "manifest," a good argument can be made that your condition was not preexisting *as defined within the policy,* especially if no record exists that you have sought medical treatment for the condition.

  Because the stakes are so high, insurers have sometimes tried to play tricky games with these exclusions. For example, they have tried to deny coverage on the basis that asymptomatic HIV signals a preexisting condition for *any* manifestation of AIDS, a highly debatable proposition under established principles of law. They have also at times argued that flulike illnesses, etc., were precursors of HIV illness, even though millions of HIV-negative Americans may have experienced the same problems. If you are confronted with this issue, seek legal help. Things can quickly get tricky.

Laws on this point vary substantially from state to state, and insurance policy provisions vary widely. Although the 1996 legislative reforms (see next chapter) may introduce some level of uniformity in defining preexisting conditions and set minimum standards for some important markets in the national health insurance industry, insurers issuing individual policies, and disability policies, will remain free to define the term for themselves. Accordingly, before you assume that the definition in the 1996 legislation will govern your situation, read the language in your policy and see whether the term is defined differently. If a conflict exists and if the definition of the term is broader than that in the 1996 law, you may have important rights under the federal legislation. If you find yourself confronted with this issue, seek legal help.

- **Waiting period.** A time, typically three months, after which an employee becomes entitled to group employment benefits. Often also known as a *probationary period*. If applicable, find out what this means to you. Similarly, HMOs sometimes impose "affiliation" periods of one month or more, during which new members are not yet covered.
- **Waiver of premium.** Typically found in life or disability insurance, in both individual and group policies. Under such provisions, insurance coverage can be kept in force *without the payment of premiums* after you have been disabled for a certain time. Check your policy carefully to see whether it contains such a provision, and if so, what its specifics provide. Sometimes, policies require that the insurer be notified within a certain time after you have become disabled in order to qualify you for the benefit. Be careful on this point.

If you are thinking about selling your life insurance (see chapter 15), the inclusion of such a provision within your policy may add substantially to its value. In calculating its "bottom line" and how much it can afford to pay you for your policy,

the purchaser should take into account that it will not have to pay premiums.
- **Evidence of insurability.** Generally, in the context of this book, being able to prove to an insurer that you are HIV-negative. Good luck!
- **Grace period.** The "extra time" you are given under your policy to make premium payments after they have become due, to keep your coverage from lapsing. A grace period of thirty days is fairly typical. If you fail to get payment to the company during that period, they will be within their contractual rights to cancel the policy. Often, even if they are bound to offer you new coverage upon such cancellation, they will legally be allowed to require evidence of insurability. If that is the case, and you are HIV-positive, you may be out of luck.

  Even if you are able to get the policy reinstated, your doing so may start the clock running again on any incontestability provisions in force. Keep those premiums paid.

  Note: If you come to realize that you are a day or two past the end of the deadline, do not automatically expect the worst. Without making any fuss, simply send in payment *immediately* and hope that they cash the check. Some companies are a little more flexible than others in sticking close to their defined deadlines.
- **Experimental treatments.** A fertile arena of AIDS-related litigation has arisen as insurers struggle to avoid payment for HIV-related treatments on the basis that they are "experimental" in nature. Since such exclusions are permitted by law, they are contained in almost every policy and have been used to resist payment for both drugs and treatments. If an insurer seeks to deny payment because a treatment is not specifically approved by the FDA, a compelling argument can be made that a more useful standard would be a showing that the treatment falls within a "generally accepted standard of care" for HIV.

National studies have shown, after all, that nearly 50 percent of the prescription drugs approved by the FDA are routinely used "off-label," meaning for purposes other than those originally intended for the drug and thus tested for by the FDA. In some states, in fact, insurers are required to pay for off-label uses so long as support exists for such use in the medical literature.

In medical care, as in numerous other areas, the challenges of HIV have pushed us to the limit. Today's experiment may very well become tomorrow's treatment standard. Realize what you are up against, but do not necessarily give up without a fight just because the treatment you are seeking is new.

A FEW POINTS ON LIFE INSURANCE COVERAGE

First, find out the amount of any life insurance you may have in place through your employment, and whether you can increase that amount without *evidence of insurability* (that means health questions or even an HIV test), or whether there may be an *open enrollment period* during which you can increase your coverage with no health questions asked. If you can afford it, obtain the highest possible level of coverage for yourself. Too often, people who *know* they are HIV-positive have failed to find out and follow through with any options they might have to substantially increase their coverage, often at minimal cost.

Second, if you must leave your employment as a result of disability or any other reason, convert your life insurance coverage to keep it in force! Realize that COBRA only requires the extension of health insurance benefits, not life or disability. Accordingly, if you fail to convert life insurance coverage on a timely basis, your rights in it may be lost forever. Never count on your employer or anyone else to keep you informed about your rights on this.

Finally, be aware that the person you have named as your beneficiary to life insurance policies will be paid the proceeds after your death, no matter what you might have provided in your will. Under some employee benefit plans, blood family members will automatically become your beneficiaries unless you specifically indicate on forms provided by your employer that your wishes are otherwise. Please do not leave this to chance. As we discussed in chapter 1, make sure that your estate plan makes sense and works together as a whole.

DISABILITY INSURANCE: A LOOK AT THE BASICS

If you ever become disabled for an extended time and are forced to rely on governmental social security benefits, you will quickly come to appreciate the role of private disability insurance in securing your future. Progressive HIV disease often leads to loss of income even as it causes expenses to increase. Some costs accrue that are rarely covered by any kind of insurance, including alternative medical treatments, vitamins and nutritional supplements, specialized professional legal or financial advice, and counseling or therapy.

Good disability coverage, therefore, intended to replace (at least in part) income lost as a result of any health condition that prevents you from working, can make a major difference in your quality of life. Understanding the specifics of any disability coverage you have in force, however, can be a real challenge. Even more than other types of insurance policies, which are often written by lawyers and therefore nearly incomprehensible, disability policies often raise special challenges.

The terms and provisions of disability coverage are not as standardized as those in other kinds of policies, making it especially dangerous to *assume* coverage until you have carefully read your policy and thought through its application to your situation. Think about it: unlike the social security disability process, defined by reams of printed guidelines, with defined rights of appeal, private disability companies have relatively few restraints. Further, if you feel wronged by their decision in your case, you may have no right of appeal other than through a lawsuit, which can be stressful, expensive, and time-consuming. Also, "disability" is not always easily and objectively verifiable, raising the possibility that your insurer may not agree that your condition makes you eligible for benefits under your policy.

If you are denied, try not to let anger cloud your judgment. If you sincerely feel that you are not able to work, do not give up. Seek an insurance counselor or other professional advice to help you put together the most effective strategy for you, and take it one step at a time.

For best results, do your best to understand your policy before you act, and to be prepared to substantiate your claim. Remember: as in successfully dealing with the Social Security Administration (chapter 12) the key is documentation of your disability. In addition to making sure *every* HIV-related symptom you have experienced is fully set forth in your medical records, it may be helpful to keep a daily journal documenting the specifics of any physical, mental, or psychological symptoms you have experienced, and the ways those problems have affected your ability to function. No matter what your condition may be, put together a strategy *now* and use it as a compass as you go.

Also, at the earliest possible time, make sure that you consult with your doctor and get his or her opinion about whether your medical condition qualifies you for disability. Do not apply for benefits and *then* find out that your doctor does not agree with your assessment! That could not only interrupt the process, but diminish your credibility when you next apply.

If you are HIV-positive and do not already have disability coverage in place, your best bet is to seek it as part of a group. Virtually all insurers now issuing individual disability policies require evidence of insurability, including an HIV test, prior to extending coverage. If you are fortunate enough to have a disability policy in place, or if an option presents itself for you to obtain one, you need to understand the basics of how the policies work, and the most important provisions to look for. Be prepared to make the best of any opportunities that may arise.

If you, like most people with disability insurance, are covered under your employment through a group policy, a tricky issue can arise in choosing the best time to file for benefits. Since such policies often offer no rights of conversion, meaning that the coverage cannot be converted to an individual policy and taken with you if you leave your job, it is important to realize that your entitlement to disability benefits may come to an end if you leave your job for any reason *other than disability*. If you feel that disability may be on the horizon for you, be aware of the ramifications that might result from your losing your job, and therefore your disability coverage.

If you have begun to seriously think about going on disability, take a careful look at your employment situation. How secure is your job? Are you possibly subject to downsizing, layoffs, or otherwise being told to move on? Is your employer a stable company that is likely to stay in business for the long term? If you fear losing your job, feel in good faith that the time may have arrived for you to seek disability benefits, and that your medical records support that conclusion, the time may have come to take action.

Before you take the plunge, make sure that no *exclusions* or *limitations* might affect your disability coverage. For example, if your policy excludes payment for any disability resulting from a preexisting condition "if the disability manifests itself within one year of the start of coverage," you are asking for trouble if you go on disability during that initial one-year period. Such provisions may be rare, but just make certain that your policy does not contain one before you take action.

If you leave your job as a result of disability, you should be covered under the group plan even though your employment has ended, because you will have qualified for the coverage at the time you were still an employee and therefore a member of the group. Read carefully any language in your policy dealing with "extension of benefits" or "when your coverage ends."

START WITH THE DEFINITIONS IN YOUR POLICY

Before you go any further, obtain a copy of your policy. If you cannot find a copy, get one, either from your employer (group coverage) or the company (individual coverage). Then sit down with your policy and evaluate the following defined terms.

- **Disability.** First, read and understand the definition of *disability* in your policy qualifying you for benefits. The best policies contain the most liberal definitions of disability, entitling you to benefits if you become unable to do *your job* or to *perform the main duties of your regular occupation*. Under such policies, it is irrelevant that you might be able to perform any other job. Next best are policies classifying you as disabled when you are unable to do your job or *any other job for which you are reasonably qualified by reason of your experience, education, or training*. This is still a fairly restrictive standard, depending on your history, level of education, etc. Finally, the worst and most limited coverage defines the term as an inability to perform *any job*. This is the standard used by social security in evaluating the question.

  Other policies base your eligibility for benefits on *loss of earnings* resulting from illness or injury and calculate benefits based upon the percentage of income you have lost.

  Sometimes, policies combine such provisions, for example entitling you to coverage if you are unable to do *your* job for the first two years, then continuing coverage for the long term only if you are unable to do *any* job. Take a close look at the language in the policy and figure out where you stand.

- **Elimination or qualification period.** In simple language, this provision tells you how long you need to have been disabled before you will start receiving benefits. Nearly all policies contain such waiting periods, which can vary from thirty to ninety days or even up to a year. Look ahead, and do your best to make sure that you have enough cash to last you until the benefits start coming in. We do not always have the luxury of being able to plan ahead, but if you do, don't squander it!
- **Waiver of premium.** Many policies provide that, after you have been disabled for a specific time, typically ninety to one hundred and eighty days, you will no longer need to pay premiums to keep the policy in force. Obviously, such provisions can be a key to making your financial picture work in the event of disability.

    Never assume that you need not pay premiums under your policy unless and until you are specifically informed of that, in writing, by the insurer. Otherwise, your policy may lapse and the situation will be ripe for conflict.
- **Your benefits, and benefits period.** In plain English, how much will you receive every month under the policy, and for how long will the insurer be obligated to keep paying under the policy, assuming you remain disabled? The benefits period can be months, years, until you reach age sixty-five, or indefinitely. Figure this out.
- **"Coordination of benefits" provisions.** Often, benefits paid under an individual or group disability policy can be part of a larger mosaic also including state and federal governmental benefits. Accordingly, disability policies often spell out how your eligibility for other benefits, such as social security, payments through other disability policies, pension payments, or worker's compensation, might affect that insurer's obligation to make payments to you. It has become increasingly common, for example, for disability insurers to "integrate" their coverage

with other benefits, meaning that your benefits are reduced to the extent you receive any other benefits, such as social security. Such a provision can cost you hundreds of dollars each month. Again, go back to your policy and figure out where you stand.

- **Recurrent disability.** HIV is not like any other illness, and even as the disease progresses, it can often result in alternating intervals of debilitating illness and dramatic remission. Consequently, a covered individual might be truly disabled at one time, but then improve and desire to return to work. Even in that event, however, the inherent uncertainty in the situation, and the looming possibility of illness, might prevent such a person from taking action.

    Since insurers obviously have an interest in encouraging such efforts, policies usually provide that if an insured person again becomes disabled as a result of the same or related causes within a certain period of time, such as six months, all *elimination* or *waiting periods* will be waived. Accordingly, since benefits will start immediately upon the resumption of any disability, at least some of the disincentive to try working is relieved.

- **Periodic reporting or exams.** Once you have been found to be disabled and to qualify for benefits under your policy, you will probably be required under the policy to submit periodically to independent medical exams, to interviews with counselors employed by your insurer, or at least to requests for written updates on your condition.

    Bear in mind that disability insurers may be approaching your claim skeptically, and they may take an aggressive posture in an effort to terminate your disability coverage at the earliest possible time even if you are seriously ill. The recent development of more effective HIV therapies, including protease inhibitors and other new classes of drugs, has also fueled the imaginations of disability insurers ready to believe that you are really *healed* and are ready to go back to work.

As a result, it is important that you find out the specifics of any reporting requirements that may apply to your case and evaluate whether those requirements are burdensome and/or may present a problem.

What about the taxability of disability benefits? Generally, such benefits are federally taxable as income only if the premiums for the coverage have been paid for by your employer, as an employment benefit. Disability proceeds typically amount to 60 to 70 percent of your salary, but reduced by taxes your take-home benefit can dip to 50 to 55 percent of your salary. To the extent that you have paid the premiums yourself, any benefits you will ultimately receive should not be federally taxable as income. Accordingly, if at all possible, do your best to make premium payments on disability coverage yourself even if the coverage is provided through your job. (Perhaps your employer can make it up to you in different ways!)

Disability coverage can be crucial in making life work for people with HIV. Treat it accordingly!

CONFIDENTIALITY AND INSURANCE

If you are HIV-positive, you know that life, health, and disability insurers are not your best friends.

The bottom line: insurance companies are in business to make money, and if you have a chronic, expensive medical condition, you do not fit into their plans. If you have HIV, you will generally be viewed by them as an unacceptable insurance risk, no matter how badly you need the coverage. It is no wonder, then, that an adversarial tension exists between people with HIV and the insurance industry, resulting in an atmosphere of distrust, fear, and secrecy. As a result, a large number of people needing testing, or treatment, fail to follow through because they fear that "the insurance companies will find out" if they seek treatment. No one is sure exactly what that means, but the idea does sound terrifying!

Important questions abound in this shadowy underground:

- If I go to a doctor for HIV treatment and run my claims through my insurance, what will be the consequences?
- If my insurance company finds out I have HIV, will they share that information with other companies? How will they keep that information, and how far can that information be spread about me without my knowing it?
- Is there a way I can find out what information, if any, is being kept about me? If they are keeping information on me, is there anything I can do about it? What if the information is incorrect?
- Is there a secretive information service that is designed to be used by insurance companies to keep people like me from getting insurance?

To get a handle on the above questions, you need to know about the Medical Information Bureau (MIB), an organization based in Westwood, Massachusetts. The MIB is an "information exchange" including about 650 insurance companies as members, including virtually all the major players in the United States and Canada. On almost every application you may complete for individual health, life, or disability insurance coverage, you will be asked to authorize the company you are applying with to check with the MIB for any records that they might have on you.

The stated purpose of the MIB is to keep and share information to help its member insurance companies detect or prevent fraud, material misrepresentation, or material nondisclosure with regard to the issuing of insurance (through underwriting) or claims filed. Here's a sample authorization, taken from an American Bar Association application for disability insurance I recently received in the mail:

> **MIB DISCLOSURE NOTICE:** *Information given in your application may be made available to other insurance companies to which you make application for life or health insurance coverage or to which a claim is submitted.*

How the MIB's Information Exchange Works

Note: Research on how the MIB actually operates can be extremely difficult, as much of the procedure is cloaked in confidentiality. I have attempted to obtain "both sides of the story" on how the MIB works from direct interviews with the company, but must point out that there may very well be a discrepancy between what the MIB says it does and what it actually does. It is probably wise to take with a "grain of salt" the explanations of its business made by the MIB. At a minimum, however, the MIB can be held to its stated rules if you are able to catch it in a violation.

The system works like this: If a member company acquires any information about you when you apply for coverage (including statements made in your application, information from your doctor, a physical exam, or the insurer's own investigation of you) indicating to them that you "have a condition significant to health or longevity," that company is required to report to the MIB a coded number that describes your condition. That's the bad news.

The specific codes used by MIB are kept highly confidential, both as a trade secret and in order to protect the confidentiality of the people involved. At least three codes are used relating to HIV:

1. *Abnormal Blood Test Result;*
2. *Diagnosis of Specific HIV Illness;* and
3. a third, more vague category relating to a *series of symptoms*

suggestive of HIV or immune disorder. (Included in this category, for example, would be night sweats.)

The first category is not HIV-specific, but includes about twenty-five other possibilities for blood test irregularities. Following input from gay activists and the National Association of Insurance Commissioners, to protect people's confidentiality to at least a certain degree, the MIB agreed not to identify an HIV-positive test result with a specific code. A diagnosis of HIV-related illness, however, is reported with a unique code.

According to the rules under which the MIB claims to operate, an insurer who obtains information from you cannot decline your application based exclusively upon the code(s) that turn up in your record. Instead, the information is intended only to trigger further or more in-depth investigation from the insurance company with which you are applying. If an HIV test was not initially required as part of the original application, one would almost certainly be required to qualify for coverage if one of the above codes came up.

The better news, and this is important, is that member insurance companies are prohibited under the rules of the MIB from reporting any information on you based upon claims you have made against health, disability, or life insurance policies. That means that, even if you are receiving treatment for HIV and running those claims through your insurance, or if you have viaticated a policy, etc., information on you should not necessarily be recorded in the MIB system. The MIB *does* offer a separate service providing information on claims filed against disability policies, for the stated purpose of "coordinating benefits" between different policies. The MIB *claims* that such information is not exchanged with its information exchange database. Thus, for example, your applying for an individual life insurance policy should not trigger disclosure by the MIB of information relating to claims made against disability policies. However, verification of the MIB's exact practices can be difficult to obtain.

According to the MIB, the only way your information can legitimately make its way into its database is if the information comes to the attention of an insurance company when you apply for a policy. Unfortunately, in applying for many policies, you have to grant the insurance company authorization to request your records for review. If HIV information is included, that *will* be reported. Also, if you test positive in a blood test required by an insurer prior to extending you coverage, for example, not only will coverage likely be denied, but (as a double whammy!) the MIB *will* have a file on you. That can definitely work against you in the future.

If an insurer requests an MIB report on you after you have applied for coverage or filed a claim, and that information is inconsistent with what you have said on your application, the information triggers further investigation, lab tests, etc.

OTHER FUNCTIONS OF THE MIB

Beyond its "information exchange," the MIB offers some additional services to its members. First, it offers a Health Claims Index, which is designed to bring to the attention of member disability insurance companies people filing claims for benefits with numerous companies. The stated purpose of the service, which keeps records of the companies and dates on which disability claims were filed, is to allow the coordination of benefits between different policies. It may also, however, trigger further investigation if the individual's "overinsurance" suggests fraud.

The MIB also provides its member companies with information on any applications you have made for insurance, for the alleged purpose of identifying individuals seeking "overinsurance" or "coverage beyond their reasonable needs." Since overinsurance suggests to insurers the possibility of fraud or other problems, further investigation may be required on your application if your name does come up.

The MIB denies keeping records of applications withdrawn, per se. Nevertheless, it does point out that if reportable information has come to the attention of the insurance company at any time during the application process, the company has a duty to report that information to the MIB whether or not the application is withdrawn. Before you authorize release of your medical records or agree to submit to a blood test when applying for insurance, think it through and make sure you understand the consequences of your actions. If you are not sure of your HIV status, get tested anonymously.

So What Can You Do About It?

If you are applying for individual coverage and the MIB has accurate information that you are positive, there's not a lot you can do. But there may be a couple of rays of hope.

First, understand that the MIB does not generally come into play with *group* insurance coverage, in which health questions are often not asked. The MIB deals with the underwriting of individual policies, in which insurance companies evaluate whether they are willing to extend coverage to you standing alone. What is the obvious implication? If you are positive, and the MIB has a record of that (we'll get to that a little later), point yourself toward a group, if at all possible, as your best bet to get covered.

Second, realize that, at least according to the MIB, any records kept on an individual are automatically deleted after seven years.

Third, even if the MIB has information on you that is correct, you *may* be able to get that information deleted if it was reported in violation of the MIB's own rules. Which leads to our next section.

Finding Out Where You Stand

The MIB currently has files on about two of every ten applicants for insurance. Before you apply for insurance, it might be a good idea to find out for sure whether you are one of those people. You can find out by simply requesting the information and sending an $8 fee, to MIB, P.O. Box 105, Essex Station, Boston, MA 02112. (There is no charge for obtaining your report if you have been denied insurance coverage within the last thirty days.) Alternatively, you can call the MIB at (617) 426-3660 for more information.

If information has been reported on you, that information will be decoded and mailed to you, along with the identity of the company that reported the information. If, after you receive your report, any information is incorrect, or was wrongly reported as a result of claims made by you on your health or disability policies rather than as a result of your applying for insurance, you have the right to request that that information be corrected, deleted, or changed.

And once again, if you are positive, don't give up. It is not an easy challenge, but be as creative as possible in seeking coverage wherever you might find it.

11

Focus on Health Insurance: Access to Coverage and Quality of Care in Changing Times

As we are all aware, those covered by health insurance often receive a dramatically higher level of care than those without. People dealing with later-stage HIV, and especially AIDS, rarely have the money to pay for expensive medications and for the top-notch, specialized medical care required by the disease. With HIV, lack of health care often translates directly into more illness, more serious consequences from that illness, a higher level of stress, and a generally lower quality of life.

Be very skeptical of any social workers or case managers whose first instinct it is to have you "spend down" your assets to qualify for Medicaid coverage. Medicaid coverage might be better than nothing, but it is no substitute for private health insurance coverage if you can possibly get it or keep in place what you already have. If you become ill and find Medicaid your only source of coverage, you will quickly realize that you can be denied certain necessary tests and procedures, and access to the best doctors. Your health can seriously suffer as a result.

Even if you have medical coverage in place, it can be a real challenge to ascertain the specifics of how your policy will work for you. Let's look at a few basics.

- What are the maximum benefits available under the policy? This is the maximum amount the insurer will be obligated to pay on your behalf under the policy, even if your medical needs con-

tinue and costs continue to rise. Is the amount in your policy likely to be sufficient to meet your needs over the long term?
- What are your obligations to contribute "out of pocket" toward the cost of your medical care, in the form of deductibles, coinsurance payments, prescription drug surcharges, etc.? What is your *stop-loss* figure, meaning the figure above which you will have no further obligations to make out-of-pocket contributions? Will your cash flow allow you to make the payments that will be required until you reach that point?
- Find out whether your policy will pay for unlimited prescription drugs. Are limits imposed on hospitalizations or doctor's visits? Is home health care covered, and to what extent? Is counseling or psychotherapy covered? How about hospice care? Does it provide for any options to keep you covered in the event of disability?

BASIC OPTIONS IN COVERAGE

There are two basic routes of access to insurance coverage: group and individual. Although there may or may not be significant differences in benefits once the coverage is in place, there are major and important differences in how the types of coverage are issued. That difference comes down to the use of individual underwriting by the insurance company when evaluating your application for coverage as an individual. In deciding whether you are an acceptable risk for coverage (i.e., whether they are likely to make or lose money on you), insurance companies will ask you questions about your medical history, possibly review your medical records, and possibly require an HIV test. Since a prospective insurer is analyzing its risk in insuring you on an isolated basis, it quite naturally becomes *extremely* interested in the details of your specific situation.

Obviously that can be bad news for the HIV-positive. Group coverage, in contrast, may be your best bet for getting covered. Even with groups, insurance companies remain concerned about the risk of claims they may be assuming, but their focus shifts and their guiding principle generally becomes one of *risk spreading* rather than consideration of individuals. The larger the group, the more comfortable insurers feel that any heavy claims experience from a few individuals is likely to be offset by the general good health of the group. Some large groups, for example, may not exclude coverage for *preexisting conditions,* while such provisions are generally the rule in the industry. The smaller the group, however, the more the insurer is likely to take a keen interest in the health of its individual members.

Your best bet to get covered, then, often involves becoming part of a group. Let's take a look at some important changes to the law resulting from the 1996 federal health insurance reforms.

THE 1996 FEDERAL HEALTH INSURANCE REFORMS: WHERE DO YOU NOW FIT INTO THE PICTURE?

Despite months of partisan bickering in the 1996 Congress, during which many feared that any legislative efforts at health care reform might fail, the Health Insurance Portability and Accountability Act of 1996 was finally passed. Although the law falls short of what it might have been, doing little or nothing for the millions of Americans lacking group coverage and therefore uninsured, it represents a substantial step forward for millions of others. If you are HIV-positive and are either currently or have recently been covered through group health insurance, the law offers you some powerful protections, and you need to understand what they are.

If you are one of the thousands of HIV-positive Americans insured through group health plans, or potentially able to join that category, these health insurance reforms could change your life. If you are HIV-positive, you understand well how precious health coverage really is, but you also know that life offers few guarantees, especially in today's business market. Coverage today does not necessarily mean coverage tomorrow, and pitfalls abound. What if you change jobs, whether voluntarily or not, and become subject to new preexisting condition exclusions? What if your insurer decides to cancel or not renew your group or individual coverage because of the high cost of your HIV-related treatments? What if your employer, or its insurance company, refuses to cover you in the first place because of your health status?

The law offers powerful protections on these points, both on the group and individual coverage levels. Under the definitions contained in the law, the group reforms generally apply to employment groups of two or more people, and apply to governmental and church groups, as well as standard business-related groups. The provisions of the law concerning *guaranteed availability of group coverage to employers,* however, apply only to "small groups" of between two and fifty members. The group market reforms apply to group plan years beginning after June 30, 1997. A key question, then, is exactly when your employer's plan year begins. Do not necessarily assume that the reforms will automatically be in place after that date.

The effective date for the *individual* market reforms is easier to figure out, July 1, 1997. After that date, all individual market reforms will be in place.

Attacking the "Preexisting Condition" Problem

One of the most serious problems facing people with HIV, or any other significant health challenges, has been "job lock." Recognizing the crucial importance of health insurance coverage, people have been afraid to change jobs for fear of losing their coverage altogether, or out of concern that the imposition of preexisting condition limitations or exclusions through the new employment could result in a gap in coverage. As you know, if you are currently on drug therapy for HIV, particularly protease inhibitors, you cannot afford any such gaps in coverage. Getting off prescription drugs, once you have begun, can lead to potentially serious problems with drug resistance. HIV takes no vacation.

Thus, thousands of people with health problems have remained in jobs in which they are not happy or failed to pursue better business opportunities, for fear of losing their coverage. The 1996 legislation deals effectively with this problem. It enhances portability of insurance by imposing important legal restrictions on the use of preexisting condition limitations by group plans and insurers. It both limits the length of such exclusion periods *and*, most importantly, gives people full credit (under some circumstances) against the exclusion period for time they have been covered by other insurance. In other words, if your insurance coverage has remained in place and unbroken (through whatever job or jobs) for at least the prior twelve months, there should be no break in coverage once you start a new job and become covered under a new plan.

The law works like this. First, it limits the time for preexisting condition exclusions (exclusion periods) in group plans. For new employees, exclusion periods cannot last more than twelve months from the starting date of employment. If you are a "late enrollee," however, meaning that you had no other coverage in force but declined the coverage anyway, or failed to take advantage of an open enrollment period, your exclusion period could legally last up to eighteen months. Keep your eyes open, and do not let the opportunity for coverage casually pass you by!

Further, the law's definition of *preexisting condition* is fairly restrictive, requiring that "medical advice, diagnosis, care or treatment was recommended or received within the 6-month period" prior to employment. In other words, no exclusion can be imposed at all unless you have received medical treatment for your HIV within the above time frame. In the absence of such treatment, and documentation thereof, your being HIV-positive should not be defined as a preexisting condition.

Second, and here is the most important innovation in the law, the length of your exclusion period is reduced, month for month, by any periods of "creditable coverage" in which you previously had insurance. The idea behind the law is that, assuming you have had no substantial breaks in coverage as you move from job to job, you should experience no gaps in coverage as a result of preexisting conditions upon starting a new job. To understand how the law accomplishes that goal, you need to understand the concept of *creditable coverage*. To put it simply, that term means prior health coverage of virtually any kind, including coverage through a group plan or otherwise, COBRA coverage, Medicare (Parts A or B), Medicaid, a state health-benefits risk pool, or other coverage, so long as no gap in coverage has occurred lasting *sixty-three days or more* between your last coverage and enrollment in your new health plan.

Are you confused yet? Let's take a look at some examples to clarify:

> Harold has been out of work and uninsured for the last year and gets a job with a new company. He has no creditable coverage in place and will therefore be subject to the maximum one-year exclusion period. During that time, his HIV-related expenses will not be covered.
>
> Rosa is HIV-positive and has been receiving medical treatment for several years. After three years of working for Acme Bakery, she is laid off. She then immediately exercises her COBRA rights to keep her coverage in place, paying the premiums herself. Ten months later, she finds a new job offering good health insurance coverage and signs up right away. Even if the new company imposes an exclusion period, it will not affect Rosa, as she will be given full credit for her years of creditable coverage.
>
> Kathy is hired as a nurse in a hospital emergency room. After eight months on the job she tests HIV-positive and

starts receiving medical treatment. Within a couple of weeks, she decides to leave and look for a less stressful job. Within a month she finds a new job teaching yoga. The new job offers insurance, but excludes preexisting conditions for the first year of coverage. Kathy will be given credit for eight months of creditable coverage, thus limiting her effective gap in coverage to four months.

Gary has been consistently covered through his group coverage at work for four years. He leaves his job and fails to exercise his right to continuation coverage under COBRA. After sixty-three days has passed, he loses any rights he had to creditable coverage. If he gets a new job and becomes covered by a new group, he will have to abide by the one-year exclusion period if one is imposed.

Take the time to figure out where you might fit in.

IF YOU FAILED TO ELECT COVERAGE AND NEED IT NOW

To further enhance the availability of coverage, the law requires "special enrollment periods" for employees who declined group coverage the first time around, under certain circumstances. If you declined coverage because you were covered as a dependent under another group plan, or because you were covered under COBRA continuation coverage, and that other coverage has come to an end, you may have the right to request enrollment in your employer's group plan. You must, however, request enrollment in the plan not later than thirty days after your other coverage has come to an end. Again, keep your eyes open, and do not let this opportunity pass you by.

GROUP COVERAGE: FOCUS ON AVAILABILITY AND ACCESS

On another front, the law offers powerful protections against discrimination by *group plans* and *health insurers* against people with health conditions. It prohibits rules restricting eligibility for coverage, or affecting continued eligibility of those already covered, based upon any of the following factors: *health status, medical condition (including both physical and mental illnesses), claims experience, receipt of health care, medical history, genetic information, evidence of insurability, or disability.* Thus, these provisions of the law aim at improving access to group insurance by guaranteeing that such coverage will be available to you no matter what your health status.

Further, group plans or insurers are prohibited from charging higher premiums or requiring larger contributions from one employee over another, if those extra charges are imposed on the basis of any "health status–related factor." Even though *the employee* cannot be required to pay more, the law does not prohibit the insurer from charging the employer more as a result of the claims experience of the group. Thus, a degree of financial pressure may remain on the employer as a result of its less healthy employees, and that reality may ultimately come back to haunt ill people covered through a group when their needs clash with the employer's bottom line.

Although this provision of the new law is extremely beneficial and important, it does not extend as high a level of protection as might appear at first glance. First, the law specifically states that its intention is *not* to require group plans to provide any specific benefits, or to provide a higher level of coverage than they already do. In other words, the purpose of the law is to expand coverage in group plans, not to dictate the benefits that those plans provide.

Second, the law clarifies that its intended purpose is *not* to prevent group plans from "establishing limitations or restrictions on the amount, level, extent, or nature of the benefits or coverage for similarly situated individuals" enrolled within them. For example, a plan might include lifetime caps on benefits, exclude certain types of coverage across the board, or limit or exclude prescription drugs. Even though such limitations would have a greater impact on plan members with chronic illnesses, they would still be permissible as long as they were not specifically and exclusively directed against people in that situation. Thus, for example, a plan could cap its lifetime benefits at $100,000 or limit its annual coverage for prescription drugs to $2,500, but such rules would have to apply to all of its "similarly situated" members. (Different treatment might be acceptable if the members are not "similarly situated," meaning for example full-time as opposed to part-time, or living in different geographical areas.)

In short, this section of the law leaves people with HIV better off than before in terms of gaining coverage, but does little or nothing to guarantee the affordability or level of quality of that coverage.

Group Coverage: Focus on "Renewability"

In a third area of important reform, the law guarantees renewability of coverage for employers in the group market. Historically, employers facing heavy claims experience from their chronically ill group members have feared losing their group coverage, thus creating a pressure-filled situation tending to put the jobs of those employees at risk. This section of the law will hopefully improve that situation, as it requires insurers, HMOs, and multiemployer plans to renew coverage in force under most circumstances. Coverage can only be nonrenewed or discontinued based upon one of the following: *nonpayment of premiums, fraud, or intentional misrepresentation of material fact, violation of the participation or contribution rules affecting the employer,* and certain other specific grounds. Claims history can never be a legitimate basis for the cancellation of group coverage.

Further, to add teeth to the law's goal of renewability, it contains some provisions offering serious disincentives to insurers seeking to terminate particular coverage, or to discontinue all coverage in the large and/or small markets within a state. Prior to seeking to discontinue or nonrenew coverage, insurers are subject to certain notice requirements and can be subject to various penalties if they fail to comply with the law. For example, if an insurer is permitted to drop all of its coverage in either an entire large or small group market in a state, it cannot issue any new coverage in that market for at least five years after that date.

Finally, the law also attacks the important problem of accessing health insurance coverage on an *individual* basis, rather than through a group. As you are probably aware, it has historically been difficult or impossible for people with chronic health conditions, including HIV, to obtain individual coverage. Unlike group insurance, in which the risk is spread among many (from the insurer's point of view, the more the merrier!), individual coverage has been based upon a specific assessment of the applicant's health. Thus, people with HIV have generally been out of luck in seeking individual coverage.

The 1996 legislation, however, has dramatically improved the status quo, at least for certain people. As of the effective date of the law, July 1, 1997, no matter what the health status of an individual applicant, insurers are legally prohibited from either denying coverage *or* even imposing an exclusion period for preexisting conditions, *under certain circumstances.* And what, you ask, might those circumstances be? To answer that question, we must return to the concept of "creditable coverage" explored above with respect to limiting preexisting-condition exclusion periods.

Under the law, you are eligible to purchase individual coverage even if you have HIV or AIDS, so long as each of the following factors are present in your situation at the same time:

1. *You must have in place at least eighteen months of creditable coverage.* Creditable coverage is defined as in the "portability"

provisions of the law, meaning health care coverage under virtually any source, including Medicare or Medicaid. Again, however, you will lose any creditable coverage you have built up if you ever allow more than sixty-three days to elapse between coverage. Under the new law, *continuity* is the name of the game. If you lose your coverage and no other options for coverage present themselves, exercise your COBRA rights, if any. Keep that coverage in place.

2. *Your most recent prior creditable coverage must have been under a group health plan, governmental plan, or church plan.* In other words, you do not qualify for guaranteed individual coverage if your most recent coverage was Medicare or Medicaid. ("Governmental plan" means a plan for government employees, not benefits programs.) Please note, however, that Medicare or Medicaid coverage *can* count toward your creditable coverage. It just cannot have been your last coverage.

3. Further, *you cannot have been terminated from that prior coverage as a result of nonpayment of premiums or of fraud.* The law places a heavy burden upon you to keep those premiums paid.

4. *You cannot be currently eligible for coverage under a group plan, Medicare, or Medicaid, and you cannot have other health insurance coverage in place.* Clearly, guaranteed availability of individual insurance is intended to be an option of last resort.

5. *If you were offered the option of continuation coverage under COBRA or a similar state plan, you must have elected such coverage, and it has now been exhausted.* Again, you will not qualify for guaranteed issue insurance unless no other options for coverage exist.

If you do qualify for and are able to obtain such coverage, you will be protected by important provisions of the law guaranteeing the renewability of the coverage, similar to the provisions affecting the group insurance market. In other words, if you fit into this part of the picture, and meet your basic obligations to pay premiums, refrain from fraud, and remain within the geographical service area (if such restrictions apply to your plan) you should be in good shape.

Encouraging State Health Insurance Reform

The 1996 health insurance reform legislation, as outlined in the preceding sections, is best understood as a "floor" for acceptable health insurance practices. To the extent the laws (or insurance practices) of your state fall short of the requirements of the federal legislation, they cannot stand. As the federal law makes clear, however, states are actively encouraged to provide their residents with a higher degree of protection, and to experiment with health insurance innovations that might better address local challenges. Many states have previously tackled the issue of insurance reform and experimented with a variety of solutions to the problems confronting them.

The 1996 legislation imposes minimum standards for state legislation, but otherwise gives states free rein. By providing a higher level of protection for their residents, states are given the choice of "opting out" of the federal provisions. Some of the possible state reforms mentioned in the law include *health insurance coverage pools or programs (often known as high-risk pools), more generous portability rules (for example, permitting larger gaps to keep creditable coverage in place), mandatory group conversion policies, guaranteed issue of one or more forms of individual policies, a mechanism for open enrollment,* or any combination of the above successfully meeting the purposes of the 1996 legislation. Find out if your state has taken any such action.

Only time will tell, but it appears that we have finally made some forward motion with respect to addressing the serious problem of access to health care, on a national level. We can only hope that, in time, the millions of Americans who remain uninsured, and therefore currently out of the picture, will receive the quality of health care that is their basic right.

On Keeping Your Health Insurance and Your COBRA Rights

If you have insurance coverage in force, COBRA might be one of your best bets to keep it that way. COBRA is a federal law (passed as part of the Consolidated Omnibus Budget Reconciliation Act of 1985) forcing employers of at least twenty people to allow their employees, and/or their dependents, to remain covered as part of the group for a certain time after they would otherwise no longer qualify for the coverage. Congress found that people were losing their employment-related coverage for two primary reasons: (1) they had left their jobs, been fired, or reduced to part-time status by employers seeking to reduce their overhead; or (2) they had been covered as dependents of the working employee, whether as spouse or children, and their coverage had been terminated as a result of divorce, the death of the worker, or the children's reaching adulthood.

The law deals with those problems and represents Congress's effort to shift the cost of health care coverage, at least in part, to private employers and insurers rather than the government-sponsored Medicaid programs. To help people keep their coverage, Congress redefined "covered employee" to allow certain categories of covered individuals to remain covered as part of the group plan much longer than they otherwise would have.

Here's how it works. If your company has at least 20 employees and offers a group health insurance plan, you have the right, when employment ends, to keep the coverage in place for an additional eighteen months. (Spouses and dependents of employees also have rights to continuation of coverage, often for a total of 36 months.) This is true whether you voluntarily leave the job, are fired, or laid off. (The rights are lost, however, if you are fired for "gross misconduct," a term that has been interpreted as requiring a showing of "willful intent" on the employee's part to damage the company.)

Your employer is legally required to provide you with written notice of your COBRA rights within 45 days of your having left the job. Although you should grab the opportunity right away, you have sixty days to choose whether to keep the coverage, and an additional 45 days to pay the premiums retroactively in order to keep the coverage in force. **An important note:** if you left your job and your employer was required to provide you with notice and failed to do so, and you are currently without other insurance, you may have important legal rights. First, politely let the company know that you would like to exercise your COBRA rights, and see what happens. If all else fails, find an attorney to write them on your behalf.

During the period of COBRA continuation coverage, however, it remains your responsibility to continue paying the premiums. By law, the monthly premium paid by the continuee cannot exceed 102 percent of the "actual cost" to the company to keep that person covered under the group plan.

Exactly which benefits are kept in force under COBRA? Any *health, dental,* or *vision* benefits currently given to the company's employees. Other group benefits, though, such as life and disability insurance, are not required to be kept in force under COBRA. (COBRA relates strictly to the extension of *health* insurance.) COBRA *only* requires that your employer make available to you the same health insurance benefits offered to its current employees. If the company drops coverage for everyone or goes out of business, your rights to continuation coverage under COBRA are lost.

Make sure your monthly premiums are paid by the due date. Although generally a thirty-day grace period is allowed, if payment is not made during that time, the policy can be canceled, and you will not be able to get it reinstated. Accordingly, try to have in place a plan, whether through a power of attorney or bank account planning, to have the premiums paid even if a temporary illness keeps you from making them yourself. You do not want to come home from a long hospital stay only to receive a letter notifying you that the COBRA coverage has been canceled.

Usually, employees have not had to pay their own premiums (if the health insurance is one of the perks of the job), and it may be a shock to you to have to pay $200 to $500 a month to keep the coverage in place. Do not be penny wise and pound foolish, even if you feel your health is stable. Beg, borrow, or whatever to get the money and *keep that insurance in place.* Otherwise, your health might prevent you from getting coverage when you need it most.

If you feel it's a stretch to pay those premiums, think for a minute about how much tougher it's going to be to pay for good medical care, prescriptions, etc. And think how your care might suffer.

Funding may be available locally to help you pay those premiums. Some states have responded to the crisis creatively by putting into place programs either contributing to or paying for people's COBRA premiums. They realize that it is much easier to pay the amount of the monthly premium to keep a private policy in force than to assume full financial responsibility for the person's AIDS care in a public hospital. Refer to appendix B at the end of this book, and call an AIDS services organization in your state to find out whether such a program may be available to you.

A Hole in the COBRA Safety Net

Please note that, under federal law, the right to COBRA coverage is available only to people working for companies with at least twenty employees. Unfortunately, a large number of Americans are either self-employed or work for small businesses and will not be protected by the federal law. Be aware, however, that some states have in place "mini-COBRA" laws, requiring smaller employers to extend to their employees analogous benefits. Check whether you live in one of those states.

Alternatively, your best bet might be to explore *conversion* of the policy. We will explore that option later in this chapter.

Note: Bear in mind that COBRA only sets forth the legal minimum with which employers of a certain size are forced by the law to comply. If you are fortunate enough to enjoy a close relationship with your employer, no matter what the size of the company, why not ask them for permission to remain covered as part of the group indefinitely? Depending on the circumstances, and your employer's conscience, they might be willing to work with you on that basis and may even be willing to help you out with the premium. It never hurts to ask!

If you pursue this strategy, however, be aware that your employer may run into problems with the insurance company if it fails to inform them of any such arrangement.

COBRA AND DISABILITY

If you leave your job as a result of disability, the COBRA rules change in some important ways. If you meet the requirements of the law, you will qualify for an additional eleven months of coverage beyond the original eighteen, totaling twenty-nine months. The extra time is intended to keep you covered until you qualify for Medicare coverage, which should be twenty-nine months after the starting date of your disability. (Since you qualify for Medicare coverage after you have been receiving social security disability benefits for two years, and those benefits start after a five-month waiting period, twenty-nine months should be sufficient to get you to Medicare.) During the additional extension period, however, you can legally be charged by your employer 150 percent of the ordinary premium. Even at that price, however, the coverage is an excellent value.

If you are forced to leave your job as a result of disability, use extreme caution in making sure that your rights are protected. As usual, the burden falls on you to make sure that you have taken all actions necessary to preserve your rights to that precious extra 11 months. How can you do that? First, understand that your right to the extra time completely depends upon the date that the Social Security Administration finds you to have been disabled. (In the "Disability Report" form you will complete while applying, look carefully at question number 3A, asking *"When did your condition finally make you stop working?"*)

As a result of the 1996 health care reform legislation, an important change has been made in the law expanding your rights to the COBRA extension coverage. Historically, you did not qualify for the extra coverage unless you were found by the Social Security Administration to have been disabled *at the time you left your job*. Thus, a heavy burden was placed on sick social security applicants to use extreme caution in identifying the starting date of their disabilities. If the wrong starting date was identified in the application, sick people facing long-term disability could find themselves suddenly and unexpectedly cut off from coverage after eighteen months.

Instead, the law now allows you the extra 11 months if the SSA finds you to have been disabled at any time *during the first 60 days* of your COBRA continuation coverage. Since COBRA coverage need not necessarily legally start until several weeks after you have left your employment, the law now provides you with significantly greater leeway in time. Even though it may not now be as necessary to document your disability as of the date you left your employment, you must still exercise caution in completing your social security application (See chapter 12). Just keep that sixty-day time period in mind.

An important note: despite the above change in the law, certain provisions requiring you to notify your employer when you have been found to be disabled by the SSA remain unchanged. If you fail to comply with these rules, you can lose your rights to the extra eleven months of coverage. Under the law, if you have been found to be disabled by the SSA and plan to exercise your right to the additional coverage, you *must* notify the employer (or the "plan administrator") *during the initial eighteen-month period* that you have been determined to be disabled and request coverage for the entire twenty-nine months. In fact, the law requires you to notify the employer of the SSA's determination of disability within sixty days of its occurrence, and you should abide by that requirement. If you fail to give notice within the eighteen-month period, however, the employer may argue that your right to the extra eleven months has been waived and seek to cut off your coverage, and that position would be supported in the language of the law.

Take no chances when it comes to this. Send a certified letter, return receipt requested, to your employer or the plan administrator (if different from your employer), or both, as follows:

> To Whom It May Concern:
>
> Please accept this letter as the statutorily required notice to the employer that I have been determined to be disabled by the Social Security Administration as of [date] and at this point plan to exercise my rights to any extension coverage authorized under applicable law, including the additional eleven months of extension coverage.
>
> If you have any questions, please let me know. Thank you.
>
> Sincerely,

WHEN DOES CONTINUATION COVERAGE END?

Now that we have explored the basic time periods established under COBRA continuation coverage, we will move on to another important question. At what different times may your right to such coverage come screeching to a halt? Let's take a look.

- First, if you fail to pay your premium by its due date or within the thirty-day grace period, your coverage will end. Do not let this happen! Use any means at your disposal to make that payment; there could be no better investment.

- Second, your continuation coverage will end if you become eligible to be covered by any other group policy (for example, if you take a new job and have the opportunity to be covered as part of the new group), even if the new policy is not as good as your COBRA coverage. If your new policy excludes coverage for any of your preexisting conditions, however, and your coverage would be interrupted, the continuation coverage will remain in force until that limitation expires. If the new coverage covers you completely, or if you have sufficient creditable coverage to avoid a break in coverage, your former employer will be off the hook.

  If you are covered by good continuation coverage that meets your needs, look carefully at the terms and quality of the coverage that would be replacing your current coverage if you accept the new job.
- Third, your COBRA coverage will come to an end once you qualify for Medicare coverage, whether you like it or not. Eligibility for Medicare coverage is triggered automatically once you have been receiving social security disability benefits for two years. Although Medicare coverage is generally adequate to provide decent HIV health care, the coverage has a major flaw: it does not cover prescription drugs. If you are aware of the high cost of prescription drugs, infusions, etc., that information may send a chill up your spine.

  What can you do about it? A couple of possibilities. First, you are often given the right to convert your COBRA coverage to an individual policy *during the COBRA continuation period*. (After you qualify for Medicare it will probably be too late.) Even though conversion policies tend to be expensive and offer second-rate coverage, focus on the prescriptions issue and figure out whether any limitations would be imposed on prescription drugs. It might make sense for you to convert the policy to cover your prescription expenses when Medicare kicks in.

Second, many states administer programs to help people pay the astronomical costs of prescription drugs they need but cannot afford, even if they are not completely indigent. However, financial limitations may apply. Get the information you need from an AIDS organization in your state, or through your state health department.

Third, explore whether the emerging Medicare HMOs in your state might offer full coverage for prescription drugs.

- Finally, your coverage under COBRA will end if the employer decides to stop offering its employees group health insurance, or if it goes out of business. Understand that your rights to continuation coverage only entitle you to the same coverage enjoyed by the group, nothing more and nothing less.

MORE WAYS TO KEEP COVERED

To figure out whether your health insurance coverage is likely to remain in place when you need it most, you should understand two additional rights you might have in addition to COBRA: rights of *conversion* and *disability extension of coverage*. Let's take a look at the distinctions between the concepts, and how they might work together.

A right of conversion gives you the ability to convert your group coverage into individual coverage, without evidence of insurability. A right to convert is often guaranteed by law. Unlike COBRA coverage, in which you are allowed to remain *part of the group insurance plan* after you have left employment, you hold an *individual* policy once you have exercised your right to conversion. At that point, it is just you and the insurance company.

Conversion coverage has two big problems: high cost and generally low quality of coverage. Insurers know that healthy people are likely to obtain more reasonable coverage from another source, and also that people with health problems will be attracted by the availability of the coverage without evidence of insurability. As a result, they charge more for less coverage.

When might conversion be appropriate? Basically, when you have no other choice:

- If you must leave your job but do not qualify for COBRA coverage because you work for a small company; or
- If you did qualify for the eighteen months of COBRA coverage but that period is coming to an end; or
- If you are near the end of your twenty-nine months of COBRA coverage (including the eleven-month disability extension) and will soon qualify for Medicare coverage. Remember, at that point you will lose your right to COBRA continuation, and the coverage of your prescription drugs. Check on the extent to which a converted policy from your insurer would cover your prescription drug expenses. If it makes sense for you to do so, exercise your rights to convert *before* your COBRA rights expire. Please discuss your options with a benefits counselor or other knowledgeable person in your state.

Note: Beware of deadlines in exercising your rights to conversion. These deadlines are usually set forth in your policy; do your best to plod through it and understand what it says. The time you are given in which to exercise such rights under the policy is called the conversion period. Typically, that period ends thirty days after you have been given notice by the insurer of your right to convert. *Even if you are not given notice,* however, your conversion rights will expire within a certain period of time, typically ranging from 30 days to 90 days. Please do not give up your conversion rights by accident.

Finally, let's take a brief look at the concept of *disability extension* of coverage. Under many group health insurance policies, and this may depend on the laws of your state, you have the right to remain covered without further payment of premiums for a designated period, typically one year, if you are disabled *at the time your group coverage comes to an end* (not necessarily the same time as when you leave your employment). During this time, you would be covered only for medical expenses relating to your disabling condition. (Thus, for example, your HIV-related expenses would be covered, but not medical care resulting from an injury or unrelated illness.)

How might this option relate to your COBRA rights or your right of conversion? First, you would only use this extension if you became disabled in a job that did not qualify you for COBRA, if you had COBRA rights but failed to exercise them, or when your COBRA coverage has come to an end. Remember, as long as you are covered by COBRA, you are still treated as a member of your employer's group. The purpose of the disability extension is to offer coverage only when your other options under the group have run out.

The disability extension, however, can be used in conjunction with your rights to conversion. Since conversion, by definition, involves your leaving the group and converting your coverage to an individual policy, you can exercise your right to disability extension at the same time you begin conversion coverage. Why would you do so? Two good reasons: first, it's free! No premiums are required. Second, any medical expenses paid on your behalf by the insurer under the disability extension would *not* be applied against any maximum benefit (or lifetime cap) imposed under your converted insurance coverage. Even if the lifetime cap seems like a lot of money, it is wise to give yourself as much margin as possible. There is no way of knowing the value of the HIV-related medical care you will need during your lifetime.

Read your group policy carefully and determine whether this option is open to you and may be useful to you.

LOOKING FOR COVERAGE

If you are currently without coverage but still able to work, seeking out the right group might be the best strategy for you to get covered. If you are HIV-positive, the health insurance available through a certain job might outweigh in importance the salary you'll be earning, particularly if you suspect that disability may be on your horizon. Although life and disability insurance benefits tend to be based on your salary, that is not necessarily the case. This shift in perspective, to benefits rather than salary as your priority, could open up some creative possibilities in your job search. Even if the salary is fairly low, a job bringing with it good health, life, and disability coverage could be a great find for you.

In addition to seeking membership in a group through employment, possibilities may still exist for coverage without individual underwriting through unions, professional associations, alumni associations, fraternal organizations, and other groups. These opportunities have, however, been steadily diminishing over the years as the uninsurable have increasingly sought haven within such groups.

OTHER POSSIBLE OPTIONS IN COVERAGE

If you are HIV-positive and not currently covered through your employment, things can get tough. In addition to the above, think about the following possibilities:

- First, you may be fortunate enough to live in one of the states (including for example New Jersey and New York) that require some insurers doing business within the state to offer *open enrollment* periods for people who would otherwise be uninsurable. Find out whether such a program is available within your state, and how to access its benefits.

- Find out whether your state has a *health insurance high-risk pool* available. A number of states have made coverage available to people (such as yourself) who are otherwise uninsurable. Such programs are typically run by private insurance companies, but are heavily subsidized by the state. Even though the programs have significant problems, such as high premiums (typically 150 to 200 percent of typical charges), some limitations on coverage, and sometimes lengthy exclusions for preexisting conditions when you first join the group, the coverage is certainly better than nothing. Call the office of your state insurance commissioner or one of the resources in appendix B to this book to verify whether your state offers such a plan and how it might work for you.
- A growing number of states are experimenting with new forms of group coverage designed to increase the availability of insurance to small businesses and smaller groups. In essence, these new programs aim to create new, large coalitions or alliances consisting of working individuals and businesses that would probably otherwise remain uninsured, then open up the bidding to different insurance companies seeking the business. In some states, participating insurers are prohibited from excluding individuals from coverage because of their health, but may exclude them for a certain length of time based upon preexisting conditions. After that period, however, they would be fully covered.

    If you are able to work or well enough to create a new business you may be able to obtain health insurance. To determine whether such a program might be available in your area, call the insurance commissioner's office of your state or your state health agency.
- In addition to Medicare or Medicaid funding, state or federal funds, including through the Ryan White Act, may be available to help pay for your HIV-related medical expenses. Call your

state AIDS hotline or the national CDC hotline (see appendix B) for further information. For information and assistance on Medicare and related health insurance issues, call the Medicare Rights Center Hotline listed in appendix B.

- If you are a veteran, important health coverage may be available to you. Especially if you meet the indigence criteria of the Veterans Administration, you may be entitled to hospital care, doctor's visits, nursing home care, and prescription drugs. Even if you are not indigent (defined by them as having an annual income of not more than $21,001, or slightly more if you are married or have dependents), these benefits may still be available to you, but you will be given second priority (behind the indigent) on hospital beds and will have to help pay a certain amount toward inpatient hospital care and doctor's visits, and to contribute a minimal monthly amount toward prescription drugs. No matter what your finances, veteran's coverage can be an extremely valuable safety net for you if you qualify. For more information about veteran's benefits, call the Department of Veterans Administration information line, (800) 827-1000. (Also listed in appendix B.)

- Finally, at least be aware of the "guerrilla tactic" strategy of marrying for coverage. By legally marrying a person who is covered under a group policy through his or her employment, you should qualify for coverage as a dependent without evidence of insurability. A small additional monthly premium may be required, but of a fairly insignificant amount. No laws prevent such a course of action. Further, if you ultimately divorce your spouse, you may qualify for 36 months of coverage as a divorcing dependent, if he or she works for a company subject to COBRA requirements.

Before you leap into this one, however, think through the legal and emotional consequences of the marriage, and the possibility that the move might eventually lead to discrimination against the employee spouse once you start filing your HIV claims. This might be more a concern with smaller companies. Should that stop you? Not necessarily. After all, such discrimination is illegal. Just be aware and move cautiously.

How Does Your Employer Handle Its Insurance?

Unfortunately, understanding the realities of how your group coverage will work in practice is not as simple as reading the policies. You must also look at how your employer provides its insurance coverage and understand the legal consequences of that arrangement. Here is a key question: Does your employer contract with an *outside insurance company* and pay it premiums to provide coverage for its group, or is it *self-funded,* meaning that all medical claims of its group members are paid by the company from money it has internally set aside for that purpose? This question may not be as simple as it sounds, because sometimes even self-funded companies hire an outside company to administer their plan, and sometimes companies use a "blended" approach, paying their own claims until a certain point is reached and then turning to outside insurance to pay any additional.

Why does it matter? To answer that question, you need to understand the basics of a federal law called ERISA, the *Employee Retirement Income and Security Act of 1974.* The law, probably one of the most sloppily conceived and poorly drafted federal laws ever passed, has had the unintended purpose of insulating certain employers from the insurance protections and regulations of state law. Originally intended to protect workers, the law has instead stripped many workers of existing legal protections. The insurance companies love it!

Under the provisions of ERISA, virtually all employer-offered benefit plans of any kind are automatically covered by the law, and jurisdiction is bestowed on the federal courts to resolve any legal issues arising under such plans. The law can be particularly harsh with regard to self-funded plans, which are completely exempted from any protections and regulations under state insurance law. Even though many such state regulations have historically protected the consumer, for example against discrimination, ERISA has been interpreted so as to seriously undercut those laws.

> Let's look at an example. In the past, employers seeking to cut costs have attempted to impose "lifetime limits" on their employee benefits for claims relating to HIV. In one infamous case arising in Texas, one creative employer trying to protect its bottom line arbitrarily decided, after one of its employees became ill from HIV, to impose a lifetime cap of $5,000 for all medical claims relating to AIDS. The only limit on any other illnesses, however, remained the $1,000,000 maximum benefit under the policy. On its face, the employer's policy was discriminatory.
>
> In desperation, the sick employee sued, pointing out that Texas state law (like the law of many other states) prohibited discrimination against people with HIV, and thus the employer's discriminatory action was illegal. Unfortunately, the employer had transferred the suit to federal court, as permitted by ERISA, and the federal court ruled that state law did not matter. The court held that all matters relating to employee benefits (including health insurance benefits) and group plans are "preempted" by federal law, meaning that the state laws are irrelevant.
>
> Finding no basis to declare the company's move illegal under *federal* law, the court upheld the company's action, leaving the sick employee without the health insurance coverage enjoyed by the other employees as a benefit of the job.

> That's the bad news. But there is a light at the end of the tunnel.

The good news is that the result in the Texas case would be different today. The Americans with Disabilities Act (ADA) has since become law, prohibiting such discrimination on a federal level. Further, the federal Equal Employment Opportunity Commission (EEOC) has issued guidelines indicating that such discrimination would be illegal if attempted today. Finally, the 1996 insurance reform legislation amends ERISA to put into place some important protections for group members with health conditions. With respect to ERISA, a new day may be dawning.

If you are covered under an ERISA plan, including most group health insurance plans provided as an employee benefit, your legal rights may be limited on that basis. This entire area of law is ridiculously confusing; a very good possibility exists that even your *employer* has no clue that its plan is covered by ERISA. Nevertheless, under the law, no such knowledge is necessary. They are covered automatically if they are providing coverage as a benefit to their employees, no matter how they structure their insurance.

What are the consequences of being classified as an ERISA plan? Plenty. In addition to the preemption issue discussed above, your remedies will certainly be affected by the law. If you feel that you have been wronged or deprived of your rightful benefits under the plan, you may be limited from seeking *any* relief in court until you have "exhausted any administrative remedies" set up within the plan. That means that, before you try anything else, you must first go back and seek relief from the plan administrators who you feel have wronged you in the first place.

Many employers, and their attorneys, are not aware of the protections offered by ERISA, and that ignorance can work to your benefit. Always try and keep one step ahead, although that is not an easy challenge in this area of the law!

THE CHALLENGE OF MANAGED CARE

In this era of managed care, it can be a real challenge for people living with HIV to receive the quantity and quality of medical treatment necessitated by the disease. On the one hand, some real benefit can accrue to you through the lower, negotiated prices available to you (as a medical consumer) through managed-care organizations. On the other hand, the same passion for cost-cutting can sometimes lead to potentially serious roadblocks in your access to health care. Unfortunately, the numerous cost-saving procedures used by such organizations tend to hit especially hard people who are chronically and seriously ill, including people with HIV. You may sometimes feel as though you are battling not only HIV, but also the very organization on which you are dependent for your health care. That can be extremely stressful.

Since managed care is already a fact of life for millions of Americans, however, and is probably here to stay, it makes sense to understand the basic goals of the industry, how it seeks to accomplish those goals, where you fit into the system as an individual with a chronic illness, and how you can best protect yourself and maximize your medical care. If you are HIV-positive and find yourself receiving care through a *health maintenance organization (HMO)* or a *preferred provider organization (PPO)*, you may at some point be confronted with various restrictions on your care. (For purposes of this discussion, we will refer to managed care generally as HMOs. Understand, however, that PPOs are often preferable (albeit more expensive) if available, as they offer simplified access to specialists and more freedom to see doctors "outside the network.")

If you run into roadblocks with your HMO, do not assume that you are powerless and fall into despair. Instead, take the time to educate yourself about the system and your rights as a patient and a consumer. Neither be surprised nor yield if the company initially denies you medical care that you feel to be necessary. Keep your eyes open to the basic workings of the system. Doing your best to understand the company's motivation, never hesitate to remind those making your treatment decisions that their imperative to cut costs *must* yield to your basic right to good and adequate health care.

Arm yourself with knowledge. Let's begin with a simple exploration of how managed care works.

THE BASICS OF MANAGED CARE

First, a bit of history. The industry emerged as a creative response to the financial abuses and excesses resulting from the limitless medical expenditures of the traditional *indemnity,* or *"fee for service"* form of health coverage. Although such traditional coverage had the advantage for both patients and physicians of allowing unfettered access to medical care deemed necessary, it also resulted in huge medical costs from unlimited diagnostic testing, unrestricted access to specialists, lengthy hospital stays, and the general popularity of expensive, high-tech medical procedures. As medical expenditures continued to skyrocket out of control on a local and national level, businesses and other interests seeking a handle on premium payments criticized a bureaucracy out of control and clamored for relief. The stage was set for the arrival of the managed-care industry.

To put it simply, managed care is all about controlling medical costs, and most of the industry's innovations are designed to do that. Although HMOs often vary in their specific rules, they generally control costs by requiring patients to use primary physicians within their "networks," limiting patient access to specialists, scrutinizing their doctors' treatment decisions with an eye toward detecting "overutilization of services," limiting coverage for prescription drugs, and sometimes restricting the use of certain medical treatments and procedures. While such cost-cutting techniques are unquestionably effective, they tend to hit hardest those with serious and chronic illness. People living with HIV need frequent and highly skilled medical care, often from specialists. They often require creative, experimental treatments, as well as expensive medical procedures and a spectrum of ongoing prescription drugs. As such, they present a challenge on several fronts to the guiding assumptions of the managed-care industry. While the HMO setup may work beautifully for everyone involved when the patients are relatively healthy, it sometimes falls short when seriously ill patients are involved.

Although a few HMOs have responded creatively to the needs of their HIV-positive patients, many others have lacked the flexibility to keep up with the disease, forcing their members to fight continuous and wearying battles to get the care they need. No matter what your current situation, remain aware that your medical needs may sooner or later directly collide with the HMO's desire to cut costs, resulting in conflict. Understanding how your HMO works, as well as your rights inside and outside the system, you may be more likely either to avoid any such conflict or to tilt the odds in your favor if it does arise.

Try to avoid making assumptions about your HMO coverage. First, read the fine print on your policy and do your best to understand how the system *says* it works. As a managed-care consumer, a heavy burden is placed upon you to play by the rules as you seek treatment. Is "preauthorization" required before you enter the hospital or receive treatments? How much freedom (if any!) do you have to choose your doctor? How can you verify that the plan doctors are competent to treat HIV? What roadblocks are put in the way if you desire to change doctors or if you want to see a specialist? If you disagree with the medical assessment of your primary doctor, what are your rights to get a second opinion, and who will make the final decision as to treatment? Does your plan offer any reimbursement if you see a doctor outside the network? How does the plan define a covered "emergency," meaning that the treatment will be covered even though prior approval was not obtained through the HMO? Are limits imposed on any of the prescription drugs that you may need? Finally, how much are you expected to pay for your care in terms of deductibles, coinsurance payments, etc.?

It is important that you get a handle on the above questions, most of which should be explained in written descriptions of your plan, but realize that your inquiry should not necessarily stop there. Understand that managed care can be a different world, in which things are not always as they appear to be. As we will briefly explore, HMOs operate successfully by exercising tight financial controls over your medical care at virtually every stage of the game. Although they often can and do provide good and adequate health care, the potential conflict is clear. An increasing number of managed-care organizations are driven by profit, and the more the HMO spends on your care, the less profit for its directors and stockholders.

Further, your doctor has been contractually "co-opted" into the system and may suffer financially if the HMO feels that he or she has given more services than required. Unfortunately, it can be extremely difficult for you, as a consumer, to figure out what hidden financial rewards or penalties may be affecting your health care, as HMOs often resist disclosure of such information as a "business secret" or "proprietary" in nature. Sometimes, doctors can even be penalized for discussing such information with patients.

Nevertheless, if you are concerned, do not hesitate to ask your doctor, or the HMO, about its compensation arrangements that might have a direct effect on the quality of care received by you. Although it may not be easy to get answers, it is worth a try. Let's take a look at some of the basic principles of managed care.

Primary Physician as "Sentinel" or "Gatekeeper." First, and probably most importantly, realize that managed care fundamentally changes your relationship with your primary doctor. Unlike in traditional medicine, in which the doctor's exclusive loyalty to the patient's well-being was the foundation of the system, doctors in the managed-care setting are often challenged by a deep conflict of interest. In return for receiving a guaranteed number of patients, vital in today's market, they have agreed to abide by the HMOs rules. Even if a managed-care doctor is conscientious and committed to your well-being, he or she may still be under considerable economic pressure to cut costs across the board, possibly affecting your care. The compensation received by your doctor through the HMO may be adversely affected if the HMO feels he has "overutilized services" on your behalf. The harsh truth of managed care is that, too often, medical treatment decisions are made by business executives seeking to cut costs and maximize profits rather than by doctors or other professionals on the "front lines." That can be dangerous.

In contracting with the HMO, your primary doctor has agreed to serve as a "gatekeeper" to your medical care on the company's behalf. The doctor therefore becomes the "point person" to police the HMO's cost-cutting imperative, ensuring that you do not receive unnecessary tests or treatments, and that you are not referred for expensive specialty care unless absolutely necessary. Does that mean your HMO doctor cannot be trusted to make the right decisions as to your care? Not necessarily. It does mean, however, that you should make your best effort to understand the way your HMO is dealing financially with your doctor, and how those hidden financial forces might directly affect your health care. Let's take a look.

Capitation and HMO payment mechanisms. Perhaps the essence of managed care is *capitation,* a payment mechanism through which HMOs pay their doctors a flat fee per patient per month, regardless of the patient's health. The sums are calculated by the HMOs based upon how many services a member is likely to use each month. While such arrangements can be quite profitable for everyone involved when a patient is healthy and requires only routine maintenance, real problems can result when a doctor is being paid only a fairly minimal amount to provide ongoing care to a patient with HIV-related illness.

In my experience, AIDS patients have sometimes been told by their HMO doctors, "Don't call me anymore. They only pay me so much a month to take care of you, and you've definitely used up all your time for this month." Should such conduct be tolerated? Absolutely not. A formal complaint should be filed against the doctor, within the HMO and perhaps also with the state department of insurance. Further, the patient should exercise his right to switch doctors. Although rarely are doctors so blunt about the financial pressures affecting their treatment decisions, those pressures are very real, very constant, and must be understood and taken seriously.

Beyond simple capitation, HMOs often place a host of other financial pressures on the doctors rendering care. Increasingly, doctors receiving larger capitation fees must pay themselves, out of fees already received, for patient referrals, diagnostic tests, and emergency care up to a negotiated maximum, often $5,000 or more per patient. Thus, in a sense, your doctor may literally feel that he or she may be paying "out of pocket" in order to provide you with the care you need. That can mean trouble. Further, HMOs often offer a series of bonuses to their doctors rewarding profitability, offering them an additional incentive to keep costs (potentially including your tests and procedures) to a minimum.

Doctors can also be financially penalized for providing you with "too much care" in terms of treatments, specialist referrals, etc. Even if they are paid through fees for services rendered rather than through pure capitation, HMOs have added an additional twist. Depending on the nature of the service, HMOs sometimes withhold 10 to 20 percent of the fee, holding that money in reserve until the end of an agreed accounting period and releasing it to the physician only if his or her total medical expenses are lower than what the HMO has budgeted for that period.

MANAGING MANAGED CARE: SOME PRACTICAL TIPS

When it comes to managed care, knowledge is power. You can receive good, solid medical care from HMOs, but you may have to work for it a little. Here are some practical tips that may be useful in choosing an HMO or in getting the best out of the one you are in.

- *Talk honestly with your doctor.* Try to get a real sense for how the doctor views the HMO. If he or she is frustrated with the setup, the odds are great that you will be also. Remember, your doctor will be your "gatekeeper" and your passport to medical care, so you must trust not only the doctor's competence to effectively treat HIV disease, but also his or her commitment to get you the care you need despite the possible obstacles.

  Ask the doctor whether the plan includes competent specialists in the areas you may need, and ask about the HMO's procedures for referrals to specialists. Ask whether patients experience substantial delays in getting to see specialists, and try to get a sense if the doctor feels that HMO procedures throw unreasonable roadblocks into getting referrals. Specifically, ask how the HMO reviews and approves the doctor's referral to specialists, as well as the doctor's treatment decisions.

  Don't waste the doctor's time; have your questions thought through in advance and write them down. Asking the right questions might provide an excellent insight into how that doctor, and HMO, might work for you.

- *Know your rights, and do not be afraid to be a "squeaky wheel."* Again, start out with a careful review of your policy. Do your best to understand how your plan works, and be aware of the potential problems. Follow carefully the rules on prior authorization of treatments, etc. If you have been told a service is covered, make sure you can find it in your contract. Otherwise, ask for the authorization in writing. If a claim is denied, do not just give up. Instead, ask the physician or the hospital why that might have happened. Make sure that a proper code for the procedure in question was submitted on the claim form to the HMO, as that is sometimes the problem.

Also request a copy of your insurer's grievance procedure. In short, "in-house" HMO appeal procedures assume that you have a right to be heard, not necessarily that you have a right to treatment the way you want it. Typically, the internal review procedures take thirty to sixty days, which can be extremely aggravating if your matter is pressing. Be prepared to go outside of the system if necessary, taking your complaint to the insurance commissioner's office of your state or to your state health department. If all else fails, the option remains to seek legal counsel to advocate your cause. That should be a tool of last resort.

Dealing successfully with managed care requires a healthy paranoia, coupled with a willingness to demand good health care as creatively, loudly, and effectively as you possibly can. Protect yourself.

12

The World According to Social Security: What You Need to Know

Let's try to take some of the mystery out of the social security process.

If you have HIV, it is crucial that you become familiar with the workings of the Social Security Administration (SSA). If you ever become disabled, your entitlement to benefits will directly affect the quality of your life. Also, whether or not you have private disability insurance in force, you will probably eventually be required to deal with the system, since many private policies require you to apply for social security benefits after a certain time. (Often, private policies allow the insurer to reduce the amount of the monthly payment paid to you by the amount you receive from social security.)

Even though the social security system can at first seem intimidating, complex, and mysterious, it does work according to certain simple rules, and the greater your understanding of those rules the more likely you will be able to successfully work the system for your benefit. If you understand what they want, and give it to them, you will be more likely to get what *you* want.

Understanding how the SSA works, however, can be a real challenge. The system uses a language of its own, and works according to its own timetable. Let's begin with a short glossary and timetable illustrating the most basic components of the social security system:

SSD stands for social security disability insurance. (Although most literature on social security refers to the program as SSDI, or DIB, for disability insurance benefits, we will use the acronym SSD for clarity and to distinguish the program from SSI. This information is confusing enough as it is!) The SSD program is best understood as a governmental disability insurance policy: so long as you have paid the "premiums" over time (meaning that you have paid social security taxes through your employment for a minimum number of quarters, or three-month periods, and thereby earned sufficient "credits"), the U.S. government agrees to pay you a monthly disability benefit.

The number of credits you need to qualify depends upon your age at the time you become disabled: the minimum number needed is six out of the last thirteen quarters (basically equivalent to one and a half years of working *and* paying social security taxes), and the most anyone of any age needs to qualify is twenty out of the last forty quarters (the equivalent of at least five out of the last ten years). SSD benefits can run anywhere between a range of a few dollars to around $1,300 a month, depending on your work history and your contribution to the system.

If you have paid your financial dues, the government does not care about your financial standing, and whether you are wealthy or not, you will be paid your benefits. If you qualify, you will receive your first check five *full* months after the starting date of your disability. In the meantime, however, assuming you meet certain strict limitations with regard to income and assets, you may be found to be "presumptively disabled" by the SSA and therefore eligible to receive temporary benefits under *supplemental security income* (SSI, which we will look at below) of approximately $484 per month until your waiting period is up. (The $484 figure is accurate as of 1997, but the amount is adjusted upward each year to keep up with the cost of living. Call the SSA to verify the current amount of the payment.)

Note: That is where form 4814, titled "Medical Report on Adult with Allegation of HIV Infection," comes in. Before you apply, request a copy from your local social security office. If you meet the criteria on the form, and if you meet financial limitations as to assets and income, you may be found "presumptively disabled" and *immediately* receive a check from SSI, as well as Medicaid coverage.

Two years after the date you are found disabled and start receiving SSD benefits, you will automatically qualify (whether you like it or not, as discussed in the last chapter) for Medicare coverage.

If you qualify for SSD, other members of your family who are dependent on you for support may also be entitled to benefits. For example, if you are legally married and have minor (or disabled adult) children, your spouse and the children may receive their own benefit, based on *your* work record, during your lifetime. They may also qualify for benefits after your death.

If you are truly disabled and fail to apply for social security benefits, this entitlement can be lost. The combined payments to you, your spouse, and the children cannot exceed a certain maximum, but the benefits do add up. Call the social security office near you to find out what benefits might be available for you and your family.

SSI stands for supplemental security income. SSI is a "means based" benefit, meaning that strict limits apply as to how much money or other assets you may have, and the amount of your income. You cannot have more than $2,000 in assets, not counting your home if you reside in it, your car (if regularly used for transportation to medical appointments), and a few other exceptions, and your income must be limited as well. (You cannot receive more than the amount of the current SSI benefit, plus $20. In 1997, that figure is $504 per month.)

If you are married and living with your spouse, things change a little. First, the limit on your assets is raised to $3,000. Second, the income of your spouse can be counted, possibly resulting in a reduction of your benefits or even disqualification. This is one area where same-sex or other unmarried couples benefit from their lack of marital status; the assets or property of a life partner cannot ordinarily be counted against your application.

If you have not paid in to the system enough to qualify for SSD, have sufficiently limited assets, and meet the disability standards, you will qualify for monthly SSI payments.

Unlike SSD benefits, there is no waiting period for your money. Significantly, too, you will automatically qualify for Medicaid health insurance right away. You will also then qualify for food stamps, although you will need to contact your local state subsidy office to apply for that benefit. Obviously, the value of what you are receiving far exceeds the cash amount of the benefit.

Which offers a better "package": SSI or SSD?

In certain circumstances, a person receiving SSI, with immediate Medicaid coverage and availability of food stamps, may be better off than someone with a larger SSD benefit, but forced to abide the five-month waiting period for benefits and caught in a two-year waiting period for Medicare with no health insurance.

Nevertheless, understand that even if you fail to automatically qualify for Medicaid coverage through the SSI program, you may still be able to obtain such coverage if you fall within the official poverty guidelines of your state. However, coverage will not happen automatically, and you will probably have to apply with your state health department. Check this out.

SSI and SSD are not necessarily an either-or proposition; you may be able to qualify for both. If you have paid into the system sufficiently to qualify for some level of SSD benefits, but the amount is less than the current SSI payment, the difference will be made up through monthly SSI payments, and you will immediately qualify for Medicaid coverage (if you meet the other requirements), and eventually for Medicare coverage as well (see below). For example:

> Melissa has earned enough credits to qualify for SSD, but her monthly benefit is only $220. Because she receives less

> than the minimum threshold for SSI and meets the financial criteria with regard to income and assets, she will receive an additional $284 through SSI and will qualify for both kinds of benefits. She will also qualify for Medicaid coverage immediately.

Medicare is government health insurance (run by the federal government) covering people over sixty-five, the blind, and the disabled. Medicare coverage consists of Part A, covering limited hospital care, skilled nursing care in an appropriate facility following a hospital stay, home health care, and hospice care, and Part B, covering doctors' services, outpatient hospital services, and a range of other services.

Once you have received social security payments for twenty-four months, you automatically qualify for Part A coverage without payment of premium. However, you must elect and pay a monthly premium for Part B coverage. In 1997, that premium is $43.80; check the current figure. If you elect Part B coverage, which is probably essential, the premium will be deducted from your social security check every month.

In spite of the limitations on coverage imposed by Medicare, the program generally pays its participating medical providers, that is, the doctors and other people providing medical services to you, a sufficient amount (unlike Medicaid, below) to make it likely that you will receive care of a reasonable quality. Historically, the major problem with Medicare for people with HIV has been the program's lack of coverage for prescription drugs, and that remains a real challenge. Your best bet might be a Medicare HMO, or possibly conversion of a private health insurance policy (see chapter 11). For more information, contact the Medicare Rights Center Hotline, listed in appendix B. Further, as mentioned in chapter 11, there may also be a program set up in your state, through its Medicaid program, to help pay the costs of your prescriptions if Medicare becomes your primary coverage.

For further information on the way Medicare works and how you might fit into the system, call the Social Security Administration at (800) 772-1213.

Medicaid is government health insurance (funded jointly by the federal and state governments, and run by your state) designed to protect the disabled who have minimal assets. Although this program pays less than Medicare to participating doctors, nursing home care and prescription medications are covered. For those with no other choice, Medicaid coverage at least opens the door to necessary care and prescriptions.

Unfortunately, because of the extremely low rate of reimbursement to medical providers participating in this program, the quality of care available to Medicaid patients is often substandard. You may have to complain and/or "work the system" to increase the odds of receiving the level of care that you need. It can be a real battle.

The 1996 federal legislation has completely redesigned the entire Medicaid structure. This is a time of flux; get all the information you can from the SSA, local AIDS-related organizations, and otherwise before you take action.

Getting Started and Formulating a Strategy

Now that we have defined our basic terms, let's take a look at how you can do your homework to improve your odds in navigating the social security maze.

First, understand that *being HIV-positive alone, with no symptoms, will not qualify you for social security benefits*. The question is not whether you are positive, but whether you are *disabled*, meaning specifically that you are unable to work. (Think about it: the system would go bankrupt if every HIV-positive person were entitled to benefits.) Even if your T cells are under 200, the CDC's current threshold for an AIDS diagnosis, you will probably not be found to be disabled if you are asymptomatic and otherwise unimpaired. On the other hand, if you have more than 200 T cells, but have had one or more opportunistic infections *and* you are able to document to the SSA's satisfaction how your symptoms leave you unable to work, you may well qualify for benefits. The questions always come back to these:

- In what specific ways does your HIV infection leave you unable to do your job on an ongoing basis?
- Which specific job requirements pose a problem? Does your health condition truly leave you unable to perform "any job available in the national economy"?
- How does HIV adversely affect your ability to meet your daily needs?

Obviously, developing a relationship with a doctor to help you through this process can make a real difference. If you do not already have a doctor skilled in HIV treatment, do your best to find one. To get your best shot with the system, remember that any impairments claimed to be caused by HIV must be well documented. Be as thorough as you possibly can with your doctor, and make it a point to get that information into your medical records. Ask to read your doctor's notes in your chart. Your future is in your hands, and you must do your best to see to it that you get all benefits that you are rightfully entitled to.

If you see a social security application on your horizon, it might also be a good idea to keep a diary specifically intended to document any mental or physical HIV symptoms you may be experiencing, as well as your emotional reaction to them, and how they have specifically interfered with your ability to function. Such a record can be invaluable if your request for benefits is denied and an appeal becomes necessary.

Although not required, it might also be an excellent idea to prepare for your doctor's signature and to submit with your application an exhaustive summary of your medical records organizing the information into a useful format, including such information as:

1. Your diagnosis and the date it was made.
2. A complete list of every HIV-related symptom you have ever experienced, along with the frequency and duration of each (whether ongoing or not). This should include not only any opportunistic infections, but also other symptoms, such as peripheral neuropathy, fatigue or pain, depression, severe anxiety, or disorientation. Again, focus on how these symptoms result in physical and/or emotional limitations on your ability to function. Mention specifically any limitations on your ability to walk distances, to sit or to stand, and any need to periodically lie down and rest.
3. A specific description of any drugs that have been prescribed, as well as their dosages and frequency of administration. Include any complications or side effects that may have resulted from the drugs, or combinations of the drugs, and how they interfere with your ability to work.
4. A list of all infusions or other regular medical treatments required, if any, their frequency and duration, and their effect on your ability to work.
5. A list identifying any surgeries or other medical procedures you have had to undergo, and their cumulative effect on your ability to work.

Keep in mind that documenting your medical history is important, but only the first step. The next and most crucial step is to document to the satisfaction of the SSA that these symptoms, individually or cumulatively, leave you completely unable to do any job.

For a concise summary providing insight into the SSA's approach to HIV-related disability, request from your local social security office their form 4814, titled "Medical Report on Adult with Allegation of HIV Infection." Review it carefully, especially the instruction sheets and definitions on the last two pages of the form.

This form is technically used by the SSA only to evaluate an applicant's entitlement to receive *presumptive* disability benefits. That means that whether or not an applicant will ultimately officially be determined to be entitled to SSD or SSI benefits, they may be awarded SSI benefits immediately if the SSA preliminarily determines that a "great likelihood" exists that a finding of disability will ultimately be made. Even if the applicant will ultimately qualify for SSD benefits, he or she will be eligible to receive SSI payments during the five-month waiting period, assuming the applicant meets the applicable asset and income limitations. The SSI payments will ultimately be substituted by SSD payments, after the waiting period.

You will note that the form is intended to be completed by your treating physician prior to or at the same time as you apply for benefits. Section C of the form lists a number of serious illnesses and opportunistic infections. These are representative of "listed impairments" under SSA rules, meaning that they are recognized as being sufficiently serious, standing alone, to justify a finding of total disability and inability to work. (If you look them over, you will probably agree.) If your medical records indicate that you fit any of these categories, you should be home free on your application for benefits.

Even if you have not been diagnosed with one of the listed opportunistic infections (the "lightning bolts" of HIV disability) or have not experienced any of those symptoms, such as diarrhea or wasting syndrome, *to the extent required by the language of section C,* all is not lost. You can still be found to be disabled, but the process is a little different and can be more tedious and fact-specific.

Under such circumstances, your doctor is then asked to complete section D, inquiring as to whether other manifestations of HIV infection, such as fatigue, fever, malaise, weight loss, pain, night sweats, confusion, disorientation, etc., have had a "marked" (that means a demonstrably significant) effect on your ability to live your life in any *one* of three separate areas: your *activities of daily living (ADL), social functioning,* or *difficulties in completing tasks due to deficiencies in concentration, persistence, or pace*. Again, read over carefully the SSA's definition of these categories in the form.

For most applicants, these final elements will be the key to a successful application for benefits. The SSA is interested in the *specific ways* in which your illness prevents you from functioning in one of these areas.

Before You Leap

Ideally, if you have been paying into the system and feel that you should qualify for SSD benefits, you should figure out what your benefit would be even before you need to go on disability. How can you do that? Simple. Call the Social Security Hotline at (800) 772-1213 and follow the automated instructions to receive a printout of your earnings and an estimate of your future benefits, called a form 7004. It's free, and definitely worth doing. In the tricky, uncharted waters of disability planning, it makes a lot of sense to gather as much information as possible before you need it.

Another good reason to request an estimate of your projected future benefits is to make sure that no taxes you may have paid are erroneously left off your report. Such mistakes do happen, either due to error of your employer or the SSA, and you can have them corrected if you catch them in time. Go ahead and request your report now; when you are sick and need the benefits is the worst time to try to start having your records corrected by the SSA.

Also, realize that if you are still able to work, you may be able to make a real difference in your monthly benefit by paying a little bit more into the system. Now is the time to figure out where you stand.

ANOTHER TRAP FOR THE UNWARY: SSI

We have just spelled out some good reasons to plan ahead for when you will qualify for SSD benefits. It is at least as important, however, that you know where you stand before you apply for SSI. (Afterward may be too late!) Why? Because unlike with SSD benefits, the government cares very much when it comes to SSI about both your assets and income. These are referred to as "nonmedical" criteria by the SSA, meaning that they directly affect your eligibility for SSI benefits.

Even though SSI benefits cannot exceed approximately $484 a month (again, check on the current limit), they are accompanied by Medicaid insurance coverage, and in most cases food stamps. If you have minor children, you may also be qualified for AFDC (Aid to Families with Dependent Children, popularly known as welfare), a program that is not administered by the SSA. Qualifying for SSI can result in an important lifeline.

Do not assume, however, that you will qualify for SSI without having done your homework. Extremely strict asset and income limitations apply, and if you own too much property (even by a little), or have too much income coming in, you can be cut off from benefits and find yourself adrift in stormy financial seas without a lifeboat.

Before you apply for SSI benefits, research the exact standards in force in your state, and be prepared when you apply. Unfortunately, the SSA's rules on this subject are extremely strict and offer no room for leeway. For example, if the SSA believes that the rent you report paying is below market value, it can figure the difference and treat that amount as income to be counted against you. At times, applicants who truly needed benefits have been disqualified because they acknowledged having $10 or $20 too much in their bank accounts. Don't let this happen to you; you can do without the hassle.

Also be aware that in a highly controversial move, the 1996 federal insurance reform legislation has made it a federal crime to "knowingly and willingly dispose of assets (including any transfer in trust) in order to become eligible" for Medicaid coverage. Keep your eyes open in this area; pitfalls surround you on all sides.

The Discrimination Dilemma

As one final consideration before you apply for benefits, move with caution if you feel that you may have been fired from your job as a result of HIV discrimination (see chapters 16 and 17). If you have either sued or are thinking about suing your employer, think through and discuss with your attorney the possible consequences of seeking disability benefits. Why? Let's look at an example:

> After Rob is fired by his employer, WidgetCo, he finds himself desperately pressed for cash and applies for social security disability benefits. In his application with the SSA, he identifies the starting date of his disability as the same date of his termination from his job. He then sues his former employer alleging violations of the Americans with Disabilities Act and state law, claiming he was "qualified" and able to do the job, but illegally fired because of his HIV diagnosis.
>
> WidgetCo seeks dismissal of Rob's discrimination lawsuit, arguing that since he has sought disability benefits from the SSA on the basis of his inability to work, he should not be able to claim in the lawsuit that he was wrongfully fired because he was able to work.

Fortunately, most courts deciding this issue have ruled that Rob would not be barred from proceeding with the discrimination lawsuit. They have reasoned that the findings of disability in the two proceedings are made in different contexts for different purposes, and that the finding by the SSA should not bar Rob's right to justice in the discrimination lawsuit. Although the courts have not generally expressly stated the point, they have realized that sick people who lose their jobs usually have little other recourse, as a practical matter, than to apply for public benefits.

If you find yourself in this position, think it over carefully, and if possible talk it over with an attorney familiar with the laws on discrimination before you decide on a course of action. You should, however, remain generally aware that your efforts to create a clear record of your illnesses for social security purposes could work against you in a discrimination lawsuit.

It is not out of the question to proceed with both; just think it through before you do.

Choosing the Starting Date for Your Disability

Before you walk into the social security office, you should have thought through in advance the key question of the starting date of your disability. Obtain from your local social security office and review the "Disability Report" form. Pay attention to question number 3A, asking, *When did your condition finally make you stop working?* Granted, with HIV disease and its complexity it may be difficult to pinpoint the date on which you were no longer able to work. Nevertheless, it is important that you understand the strategic significance of that date.

First, be aware that your right to continuation health care coverage under COBRA once you have left your job (see chapter 11) will depend on the date *you* identify in your social security application as the starting date of your disability. Under COBRA law, as modified by the 1996 health insurance reform legislation, employers are forced to allow you to remain covered under the group plan for an extra eleven months (beyond the standard eighteen months) only if you were found to be disabled within the first sixty days of your COBRA continuation, and the SSA determines that based upon information you provide in your application. Please see the discussion of this point in chapter 11, under the section titled "COBRA and Disability."

The starting date you identify is also significant for an entirely different reason, particularly if you will qualify for SSD. While you can never receive SSI benefits retroactively, i.e., earlier than the date of your application, you can be awarded SSD payments back to the starting date of your disability. Similarly, if you qualify for benefits, any dependents qualifying for benefits based on your record can also receive benefits relating back to that date, and that money can really add up!

Finally, realize that you will receive no SSD benefits until you have gone through the waiting period of five *full* months. Unless the starting date of your disability falls on the first of the month, your waiting period will not even start until the beginning of the next month. Be aware, then, that the date you choose could result in that additional month's delay.

Under no circumstances can the starting date you identify be more than seventeen months before you apply, adding up to one year plus the waiting period. Nevertheless, if you feel you will qualify for SSD and that you can in good faith identify an earlier date on which you became disabled, do not hesitate to do so.

Now That You Are Prepared . . .

If you have completed the above homework assignments, getting the ball rolling is fairly easy. If you are ill, weak, or find it difficult to travel, no problem. In most cases, you can apply for benefits over the telephone, and follow up by mail, without ever visiting the office. Of course, you can also set up an appointment to visit the office, if you prefer.

If you are disabled and ready to apply for benefits, call the SSA's toll-free number, (800) 772-1213, between 7 A.M. and 7 P.M., Monday through Friday, and a social security representative will schedule a telephone appointment for you with a claims representative. Getting started is that easy.

If you ask, they will tell you what documentation you should gather together and have prepared, starting with your birth certificate. You will need an original. If you cannot find it or otherwise get it in hand, contact (in this order) the hospital where you were born, that city's government, or the state's department of health. You will also need your social security card, copies of your medical records (not required, but helpful to expedite the procedure), and financial documents if you may qualify for SSI benefits, including tax records, W-2s, bank statements, etc. If you are married, the records of your spouse will probably also be required.

A Look behind the Scenes

To illustrate how the system works at its best, let's follow the case of our hypothetical friend Janice as she applies for SSI benefits. Pay careful attention to her story, because you would be wise to follow some of her actions:

> After much thought, and discussing the matter with her doctor, Janice decides that she no longer has any choice but to go on disability. After calling social security's toll-free line, (800) 772-1213, she is referred to a claims representative. To expedite the process of receiving her benefits, Janice obtains from her doctor copies of all her medical records. Fortunately, she has always communicated in full detail to her doctor and made sure that the doctor placed in her medical records a thorough record of such hard-to-document symptoms as fatigue, depression, dizziness, and mild disorientation.
>
> At the time she applies, she also provides social security with a list of the names, addresses, and phone numbers of

all of the doctors, clinics, and hospitals she has been to since her illness began.

Based upon the severity of Janice's claim of HIV-related disability and her prior illnesses, the SSA immediately flags the outside of Janice's file with an orange notice to expedite the case. Further, because she has done her homework in gathering her medical records, the file is also flagged to alert caseworkers that her medical evidence is in the file, and that the stage is therefore set for the determination of her disability.

Her file is then transferred for evaluation to a state-run agency, Disability Determination Services (DDS), which operates under contract with the SSA and is initially responsible for evaluating Janice's claim of disability. Once they have found Janice to be disabled, the SSA is notified and she receives her monthly benefits and Medicaid coverage, and she is able to apply for food stamps.

Under recent changes to SSA guidelines, additional manifestations of HIV infection specific to women, usually gynecological in nature, have finally been added to guiding standards. If you are a woman, discuss this matter with your doctor, and be as complete as possible about describing any symptoms you might have experienced. It is late in the game, but medical professionals are now beginning to acknowledge that, in women, certain problems that are not unique to HIV, such as yeast infections or cervical problems, can signal HIV-related illness. Talk this over with your doctor, and make sure that your medical records are complete.

WHAT IS A TRIAL WORK PERIOD?

What if at some future point your condition improves and you regain an ability to work? Will you automatically lose benefits by pursuing any such opportunity? Not necessarily.

More than many other illnesses, HIV disease often involves intervals of disability and improvement. If one feels able to return to work, even if on a trial basis, definite psychological and financial benefits can result. To encourage such experiments, the SSA has established a fairly liberal trial work program.

At any time after you have been found disabled by the SSA, you are free to return to work for a period not to exceed nine months without affecting your benefits. That nine-month total does not have to be consecutive, but can be flexibly structured in whatever intervals best meet your needs. Further, during the trial period, you are permitted to earn any amount of money without affecting your benefits.

For more specific information on this program, contact your local social security office or call the national hot line and request the SSA's pamphlet on the topic. Evaluate whether such an experimental work program might fit your needs.

A Look at the Social Security Appeals Process

Even if you are truly sick and unable to work and take all the right steps in preparing and submitting your case to the SSA, your application may still be denied, leaving you with no benefits.

A denial of benefits is not the end of the world, but it might feel that way. The first enemy you will have to face will be time: an appeal will take several months and often more than a year. During that time you will not automatically qualify for Medicaid and other poverty-based benefits that would accompany a finding of disability by the SSA. Further, once you have been denied, any presumptive benefits you may have been receiving will suddenly stop. All of that can be extremely frustrating.

That's the bad news. The good news is that a large number of denials of HIV-based disability claims are reversed during the appeal process, mostly at the *administrative hearing* stage (see below). If you have been denied benefits, it is essential that you understand the basics of the SSA's review system and figure out how to take your best shot at achieving a positive result.

Should you use an attorney? You are not required to during the appeals process, but you should seriously think about retaining one. Expert advice can definitely make a difference in the results of your case. A successful result boils down to two basic factors: an understanding of what the SSA is looking for in your application or in your appeal, and an understanding of how to give it to them. The right attorney can help clarify those issues for you.

How are such attorneys paid? Typically, you need not pay for attorney's services "out of pocket." Instead, you must be willing to share a percentage of your recovery with the attorney in return for his or her efforts. The standard fee is 25 percent of the *retroactive* benefits recovered, meaning the benefits you are awarded spanning from the date you are ultimately found by the SSA to have been disabled to the date that the determination is made. Let's look at an example:

> Katrina originally applied for SSD benefits in January 1995, alleging her starting date of disability as September 4, 1994. In March 1995, she is denied benefits. Her appeal is ultimately concluded in January 1996, and she prevails. She is awarded retroactive monthly benefits of $750 for the eleven months between the conclusion of her waiting period and January 1996. (Remember, her five-month time clock started running on October 1, 1994, the next *full month,* and ended on February 28, 1995.) Accordingly, the SSA finds Katrina entitled to $8,250, 75 percent of which ($6,187.50) is immediately released to her. The remaining 25 percent is held by the SSA for the benefit of Katrina's attorney.

Before you hire an attorney, try to interview several to explore different possibilities. Don't be afraid to ask specific questions about their experience in social security appeals (if not *HIV-related* social security appeals), and to ask exactly how your case will be handled and the length of time you should expect from start to finish.

A referral network has been established by the National Organization of Social Security Claimants' Representatives to facilitate your connection with attorneys in your area who are experienced in social security appeals. (See appendix B). If you feel uncomfortable with an attorney you have met with or doubt his or her competence, honor your instincts and move on to the next possibility.

Depending on the specifics of your case, you may be better off using an attorney, even though doing so will ultimately reduce the amount of benefit coming to you. The process can be complicated, and getting your point across on appeal in a direct, professional, and competent manner can make all the difference. Also, having an experienced professional on your side can reduce your stress. Before you decide, at least carefully read over the following description of the appeals process and think honestly about whether you can do it on your own and do it right.

The four stages of review are (1) *reconsideration,* (2) *administrative hearing,* (3) *Appeals Council,* and (4) *federal court.* At each stage, the only question of relevance is whether or not you are disabled *and* unable to work at any job. You will argue that you meet that standard, and the SSA will beg to differ. So begins the dance.

If you are denied the first time around, the next step will be to request *reconsideration* by the agency that originally made the finding, the DDS. Though relatively few reversals are made at this level, it is wise to take it seriously, because you never know! Understand that the DDS, the first time around, was not convinced that the HIV-related symptoms you described were sufficiently serious to leave you unable to work. View this stage as your first opportunity to make that more clear.

Documentation is all-important at this stage. Often, months will have elapsed between your original application and your request for reconsideration. Make sure that your medical records are brought up-to-date and supplemented, and fully expand on any functional or medical decline that might have developed in the interim. Also, ask your doctor to write a narrative explaining how your symptoms taken together limit your ability to function.

Once you have been denied, you have sixty days to seek reconsideration, and the clock starts ticking five days from the date of the original notice that you have been denied. Move on it as quickly as possible; it will get you that much closer to your ultimate goal. If you fail to file on time and are unable to show "good cause" why according to SSA guidelines, you will have to file a new application and start the process all over. This can be especially devastating if you are applying for SSI, because you can only be awarded such benefits from the date of your application, and the new filing will start the clock anew.

If you are applying for SSD, however, a new start is not quite as disastrous, because your benefits (assuming you eventually qualify) will depend on the starting date of your disability, which can be the same in the new application as it was in the old.

THE NEXT STEP: ADMINISTRATIVE HEARING

If your request for reconsideration has been denied, you should immediately request a hearing before the administrative law judge (ALJ). Depending on which part of the country you live in, and the size of the backlog of disability cases there, it can take several months to get a hearing. Move as quickly as you can, but have a strategy in place.

Unlike the prior stage of review, these hearings are held before independent ALJs who work for the SSA's Office of Hearings and Appeals (OHA). Although some important differences exist between these hearings and court proceedings, the best way to approach them is as a full trial on the issues of your disability and your inability to work, in which the ALJ sits as your judge and your jury. The burden is on you to prove your case and to convince the ALJ that Disability Determination Services was wrong in its determination.

Unlike in trials, no attorney is fighting you on the other side, and the rules of evidence are considerably relaxed compared to court proceedings. For example, "hearsay" evidence is allowed, meaning written statements by people who are not present in the courtroom and are not subject to cross-examination. Thus, affidavits from professionals, neighbors, etc., can be submitted, as well as your medical records. At this stage, your task is to use every tool at your disposal to create a clear record of your inability to work as a result of your HIV infection.

If you have requested a hearing before an ALJ, you (and your attorney, if you have retained one) are notified by OHA when the file has been delivered to them. Once the file has been organized by OHA personnel for the hearing, you have the right to review and copy it, if you wish. That is only the starting point. Prior to the hearing (which takes place months after you requested it), it is crucial that you make sure that your file is supplemented with fully current medical information, and also psychological information if applicable.

With HIV, disability can result from physical, mental, or emotional symptoms, or a combination of all three. Do not omit any details of any ongoing fatigue, depression, anxiety, disorientation, or any signs of dementia you might have experienced. At all times, make sure that you have kept your doctor fully informed as to any such symptoms, and that comments have been written accordingly into your medical record.

It is also a good idea to prepare and submit a *prehearing memorandum* outlining the evidence and identifying the issues for the hearing. Such a memo, properly prepared, could do much to distinguish your case from the dizzying number of other cases currently before your ALJ. The memo should be submitted to the ALJ several days before the hearing. All evidence and the records on which you intend to rely should ideally be submitted in advance of the hearing, but can be submitted on the day of the hearing if necessary. Remember, this is your best shot. Proceed with deliberation, forethought, and caution.

Each ALJ is different and runs the courtroom his or her own way, but here are some guidelines. The hearings are generally informal, recorded by tape recorder rather than a court reporter. Since there is no attorney on the other side to cross-examine you, the proceedings often start with the ALJ asking you questions directly. Sometimes your attorney (if you have one) will be given a chance to ask you questions first, with the judge to follow up.

You should be prepared to testify as to your age; your education; the physical requirements of your last job, including any requirements to walk, lift, or otherwise move, including standing and sitting; and also about any HIV-related mental or emotional conditions that might keep you from working, such as fatigue, depression, or disorientation. In short, be prepared to convince the ALJ as to exactly why you are unable to work.

Your attorney may want to call witnesses. The hearings are generally limited to not more than two hours. Certain live testimony can be extremely compelling and will be given great weight by the ALJ, such as from your doctor, psychiatrist, or whoever else might have knowledge of your illness and its effect on your ability to work. Mostly, however, such testimony is submitted through affidavits, which can be helpful to the ALJ and help point him or her in the right direction.

The ALJ may require your examination by a consultative physician to get a second opinion on your disability claim. This is especially common if you have not established a relationship with your own doctor. Since consultative physicians are selected and reimbursed by the SSA, guess what their opinion often turns out to be?

You guessed it: not disabled! However, the courts have ruled that the opinion of your treating physician should be given greater weight than that of a consultative physician. If you do receive such an examination, do your best to convince that doctor of your disability. Again, do not leave out any symptoms or HIV-related problems that you have experienced. If the consultative physician finds that you are disabled, that finding may go a long way toward convincing the ALJ that your claim is legitimate.

The ALJ may announce a ruling at the conclusion of your hearing. Even if you are found to be disabled, you will not start receiving benefits (including any retroactive payments to which you might be entitled) until the ALJ's *written* ruling is released. That can often be months after the hearing. Not an ideal situation, but that's the way the system works.

The End of the Road

The final two stages of appeal, the Appeals Council and the federal courts, are only rarely used. If the ALJ denies your appeal, you can seek review by the Council, which will make a decision based on the records and transcript of the hearing, without oral argument. Appeals are rarely successful at this level.

Within sixty days of an adverse ruling by the Council, you can seek review in the federal courts. It is important that you understand, however, that federal judges do *not* reweigh the question of whether or not you are disabled. Instead, their only role is to hear any constitutional issues that might be raised, or to evaluate whether the SSA followed its own rules and gave you "due process" as it turned you down for benefits. Since the scope of federal review is so limited, this ultimate stage will rarely help you.

The moral of this story: do your very best to do it right the first time!

13

Dealing with Creditors: A Look at Some Alternatives to Bankruptcy

For the vast majority of people with HIV, living with the disease raises several serious financial challenges. Too often, as income plummets due to disability, expenses increase exponentially. Fighting the good fight against HIV requires expensive medical treatment (not to mention an array of vitamins and supplements that are often not covered by insurance), legal help, counseling, and an array of other services.

How is a newly disabled person, now out of a job, trying to pay medical bills and living on government benefits, supposed to pay off consumer debt and otherwise make ends meet? Those obnoxious calls from collection agencies keep coming, and often, even if one is committed to making good on obligations, something has to give somewhere.

Bankruptcy may be the most effective means of dealing with your financial problems. On the other hand, simpler, cheaper, and less damaging means may be available to deal with your situation. Let's take a look at some of the possibilities.

Why is it important that you be aware of some alternatives to bankruptcy? For a few reasons. First, you can only "do bankruptcy" once every six years. Second, bankruptcy is the ultimate disaster for your credit rating. People with HIV are now living longer than ever before, and keeping credit available can be an important part of your financial strategy. Third, bankruptcy may be overkill for your situation, and simpler, quicker, and cheaper options may be available to you.

For example, if creditors are hassling you, you can try the following complementary strategies: talking to them and working out a payment schedule with them; trying to negotiate down the amount owed; advising your creditors, if such is the case, that your disability prevents you from working anymore; or *threatening* to resort to bankruptcy if your creditors will not agree to work with you in reducing the amount of the debt. That can be a powerful weapon.

PUT TOGETHER A STRATEGY

In evaluating whether alternatives to bankruptcy might work for you, try not to react impulsively and emotionally. Instead, take a good, hard look at the realities of your situation. For example, don't let one or two particularly aggressive and obnoxious credit collection agencies push you into bankruptcy proceedings without first evaluating your situation. Be sure to consider the following as you ponder your direction:

1. *What is your debt situation, compared with your present and prospective income?* Is there any chance you can make the whole thing work by setting up a stricter budget for yourself? While that can obviously be difficult or impossible if you are disabled, living on a fixed income, and saddled with past debts, it may still be worth a try, especially if you are willing to try to negotiate with your creditors for reduced payment, or to waive interest for you.

   If you are going to try to pay your bills, think about seeking help from a consumer-credit counseling service in your area. Often, such nonprofit agencies offer assistance free of charge in assessing your overall financial situation (income/assets versus debts), helping you negotiate with your creditors, consolidating your debts, and coming up with a payment schedule. Think about it from the creditors' point of view: it's better that they waive interest (which they typically agree to do) or agree to partially reduce the amount of a debt rather than risk losing the whole amount if you declare bankruptcy.

2. *What are the nature of your debts? What can you expect to happen if you do not pay?* This is important for a few reasons. First, bankruptcy will not wipe out certain kinds of debts (such as child support, student loans, and a few other categories). Also, you must realize that *secured creditors* (such as holders of your mortgage, the lender on your car, etc.) must be treated more carefully than general or *unsecured* creditors. If you don't, you may lose your house, car, or other important assets. Common sense should tell you that certain debts, such as your mortgage or rent, your utility/phone bills, your car payments, etc., must take priority for you to avoid unfortunate consequences.

Of all the choices open to you as you struggle with your debts, ignoring your creditors is the worst. Sure, it's tempting to just toss those bills, but that could really come back to haunt you. There is a better way! To protect yourself in your dealings with creditors, and to stand your best chance at successfully working the system, you need to understand the legal basics of debtor/creditor rights. What can creditors do to you through the legal system to try to collect? Which of your property is *exempt* and therefore beyond the reach of creditors? Are you *judgment proof*, and if so, might it help to let your creditors know that?

CREDITORS' WEAPONS

Note: Be aware that, in this particularly tricky area, laws vary from state to state. As a result, it is absolutely essential that you seek legal advice on the specific requirements of your state. In this area, involving your basic property rights, the costs of a mistake can be high.

As common sense would tell you, the more assets you have, the greater the range (and effectiveness) of means available to your creditors to help them collect their debts. Depending on the laws of your state, creditors may have some fairly nasty and effective tools at their disposal.

At the risk of oversimplifying a complex area of the law, you need to know about the following creditors' remedies. Some can be used before creditors obtain a judgment (but while they are suing you), while others can be used after the creditor has successfully sued you and obtained a court judgment against you. Keep in mind, though, that *secured* creditors (e.g., the holder of your mortgage, lender on your car, etc.) have other strong protections in place to help them. Do not treat those creditors casually.

Wage garnishment. Although legal limitations exist on a creditor's right to garnish your wages, this tool can be devilish. If a judgment is entered against you, the creditor may have the right to take part of your wages from every check. However, the amount they can take is limited, and some other exemptions may protect you in your situation. Ask a lawyer in your state.

Bank account attachment. Your account can be frozen or money taken from your account by your creditors if they get a judgment against you.

Attachment and levy of property. In the worst case, creditors who have obtained a court judgment against you can have your local sheriff levy your property, meaning take your property from you and sell it. Personal property can be sold, while a lien can be placed against your real property.

Is Your Property Exempt?

By now, you may be ready for some better news. Under the laws of every state, some important property is classified as exempt, meaning that creditors cannot use the above tools to get to it, *even if they have a judgment against you and are ready to move on it.* Some important examples:

Your home. If you own your home, that asset is usually fully beyond the reach of creditors. Not only are they prohibited from forcing a sale of the property, but they cannot even put a lien against it. (Check your state's law on this.) Even if you sell your home, the proceeds may still be protected for a "reasonable time" if you plan to buy another home with the money. (Think about it. If it's done right, you can convert nonexempt assets [such as cash] to protected status by investing them in exempt property. But please, consult an attorney or other professional before you rush into that one.)

Personal property. Your "stuff," up to a certain value, is protected. And you get to choose the property. (In Florida, that amount is $1,000. Check the limit in your state.) The limit can include a fair amount of property, at garage-sale prices. In cases involving ordinary consumers, it is almost unheard of for their personal possessions to be taken by creditors. (Usually, the cost to the creditor in such actions, coupled with the risk of nonrecovery, serves as a strong disincentive.) Also, a portion of the equity value in your car, if not the entire value, is protected.

Health-related equipment. In some states, any "health aids" prescribed by a physician, apparently of any value, are exempt. This would include wheelchairs, other health-related equipment, etc. You could get creative with this one!

Life insurance proceeds. All proceeds from life insurance (this does not include viaticated funds) are exempt. However, if you have named your estate as the beneficiary, creditors will get a chance to seek some of the funds by filing claims against your estate after your death. Be careful!

Other important exemptions you should be aware of: disability income, veteran's benefits, social security payments, and various pension payments.

If you feel that your property falls into the above categories, or if you have no property, you are probably "judgment proof" and in a position of greater strength in dealing with your creditors. (Once again, though, remember that secured creditors have extra rights with regard to the property securing their loans.) You are "judgment proof" if your creditors could not successfully collect money or property from you, even if they obtained the entry of a court judgment against you.

If health issues or other problems have pushed you into a corner with regard to your general, or *unsecured* creditors, it can be a useful strategy to inform them of your judgment-proof status. Using that strategy will definitely blow your credit rating, and would obviously affect your confidentiality to the extent you raise HIV or make your health an issue, but you may not care. Think very carefully before you move on this strategy. Times are changing and treatments are improving, and you can no longer assume that you will not be here for several more years just because you have HIV. Think seriously about trying to preserve your credit and working out a payment plan with creditors in order to preserve your future options.

If you have thought it through and decided to give up on paying your debt, and are prepared to risk losing some or all of your credit, let the creditors know where you stand. Often, creditors will not bother to proceed with collection efforts if they know up front that it will be a waste of their time and money. For example, a person dealing with HIV or other health issues could write a letter along the following lines:

A Sample Letter

Creditor

Address   Date

Re: Your Name and Account Number

Dear Sir or Madam:

    This letter is to advise you that due to serious medical problems and my inability to continue working, I must reluctantly suspend payment on my account. I am permanently disabled by [mention AIDS or HIV if you are comfortable in doing so], and [social security, public assistance, disability benefits] are my sole source of income.

    I have consulted an attorney, who informs me that I am "judgment proof," meaning that my few assets are exempt under [name of your state] law. My attorney said there should be no need for me to file for bankruptcy if you understand my situation.

    At such time as I am able to return to work, I will immediately begin repaying the debt. In the meantime, please abate any collection activities against me. I have been advised by my doctor to avoid stress and therefore ask that any future contacts be made in writing, and not on the telephone. Also, please remember that information about my medical condition is confidential, and not to be released without my specific written consent.

    If you need any further information, I will be happy to provide it for you. Thank you for your assistance and human understanding at this difficult time in my life.

Sincerely,
Frank Harris

If any of your creditors are driving you crazy and you have no present ability to make payments toward those debts, it is important that you be aware of your rights under the Federal Fair Debt Collection Practices Act. Under that law, you have the right to request that a creditor stop calling you to harass you for payment, etc. A sample letter is as follows:

Re: Your Name and Account Number

Dear Creditor:

I have received numerous phone calls and several letters from you concerning bills I have not been able to pay. Under 15 U.S.C. 1692c, this is my formal notice to you to cease all further communication with me except for the reasons and in the manner specifically set forth by law.

Very truly yours,

Mail the letter via certified mail, and request a return receipt. (That green receipt will serve as proof that the letter was delivered.) After they have received the letter, the creditor is legally prohibited from contacting you except to notify you that there will be no further contact, or that specific action will be taken. Don't use this technique with every creditor as it may be important for you to listen to what they have to say, but keep it in mind in the event you are absolutely unable to pay a bill when a particular creditor is stressing you out.

Realize the difference between this letter and the last. Here, you are forcing the creditor's hand, and basically saying "either sue me or back off." With the first, you are asking the creditor's forbearance in writing off the account, or otherwise compromising the amount due. Don't expect your creditors to be happy about either!

To sum up, you will best be able to protect yourself financially if you take a clear look at your situation, weigh the risks and benefits in the choices open to you, and make a considered decision. Try not to let the stress get to you: keep in mind that, no matter what your situation, there is a way to handle it. We are not saying it's easy, we're just saying there is a way!

14

The Basics of Bankruptcy

Never leap into bankruptcy without having fully considered all of your other options, and without being aware of its disadvantages.

Bankruptcy can be an extremely effective way of dealing with your debts, but your situation may not be sufficiently severe to call for such a strong remedy. In solving a debt problem, personal bankruptcy is the rough equivalent of a neutron bomb, when in some cases a flyswatter might do instead. One major problem is that a bankruptcy stays on your credit report for ten years. You should also realize that preserving credit (to have access to funds in an emergency) may be an extremely important goal if your future financial horizons are unclear.

Let's start with the basics. Bankruptcy is a federal court procedure (even though state law is also involved) designed to give a fresh start to debtors who have gotten in financially over their heads, by eliminating some or all of their debt.

Although there are three primary options to choose from when filing for bankruptcy, we will focus on the procedure used under Chapter 7, or "liquidation." Most individual (as opposed to corporate or business) bankruptcies fit into this scheme. Nevertheless, a quick caveat: if you are thinking about bankruptcy, you should consult with a knowledgeable attorney. Traps for the unwary abound and good legal advice is definitely worth the cost.

To illustrate, let's examine the situation faced by Mary as she undertakes a Chapter 7 bankruptcy. Now living on disability income, she has gotten herself into a financial mess, and all her credit cards are maxed so she can no longer get cash advances to pay off other debts. The calls, letters, etc., from the collection agencies are finally forcing her to break down and consult a lawyer about her problem. Given her relatively simple situation, she is quoted a "flat fee" of a few hundred dollars, and an additional $200 in costs to get the case filed in court. Attorneys' prices vary (shop around, but remember, you get what you pay for) and depend in part on where in the country you live. Typically, the attorney asks for the money up front. Mary agrees to the arrangement.

Prior to the meeting, the lawyer asks Mary to make a complete list of all debts, including amounts and the creditors' names and addresses, a complete list of all property owned by her, and a monthly budget, setting forth her recurring income and expenses. This information is needed to figure out whether Mary needs bankruptcy or not, and if she does, the type that is right for her.

Also, as the attorney explains to Mary at their initial meeting, it is crucial that Mary list every creditor whose debt she wants *discharged*, or eliminated, in the schedules filed with her bankruptcy petition. As soon as Mary files the petition, an *automatic stay* comes into effect completely preventing those creditors from calling, suing, or making other collection efforts. (Creditors will receive notice in about two weeks from the court, or sooner if they are particularly obnoxious and Mary asks her attorney to get them off her back.) Also, a *bankruptcy trustee* will be appointed to take charge of the procedure, including reviewing the petition, schedules, etc. (It is important to be nice to the trustee!) The trustees are usually accountants or other professionals, who are paid by the system and act as "officers of the court" in administering bankruptcies.

The Role of the Trustee

The attorney explains that, barring unforeseen complications, the process should take a little over three months and illustrates the procedure like this: "Once you file for Chapter 7, you put all your debts in one suitcase and all of your assets in another, and bring them both to the trustee and lay them out on the table in front of her. The trustee opens up both suitcases. From the debt suitcase, the trustee takes nearly all of your debts from you. Under the law, however, certain debts cannot be discharged through bankruptcy, such as most taxes, child support, alimony, student loans less than seven years old, and certain other special kinds of debts. These debts, and these alone, will be returned to you by the trustee, and bankruptcy will not help you with those. Also, bankruptcy will not generally protect you from secured creditors, such as those holding the mortgage on your home or financing your car.

"From the asset suitcase, the trustee will return to you certain *exempt* property, such as the home you own, one thousand dollars' worth of personal property, home furnishings, etc. [and that covers many people's property, at garage-sale prices], your car, any cash value in life insurance, retirement pensions, etc. The rest of your assets will be taken by the trustee to be distributed between your outstanding creditors." Obviously, the way Mary holds her property is crucial at the time she files. That is why it is so important to consult with an attorney as soon as you think that bankruptcy may be anywhere on the horizon of your future.

Before you leap, also ask yourself, "What kind of debt is it I'm trying to get rid of?" For example, bankruptcy will not help you get out of paying for damages resulting from your drunk driving, out of most of your taxes, or recent student loans. It makes no sense to file if those are the debts that you are trying to avoid. On the other hand, if you can wipe the slate clean of other debts, you might be able to manage the debt you can't eliminate more easily.

Think about timing, too. Is *now* the best time, strategically speaking, to wipe the slate clean? Is there a potential large and ugly creditor out there whose future claim might rear its ugly head shortly after you have gotten your order of discharge, leaving you exposed? Remember, you can only declare bankruptcy once every six years.

It's important that you realize that any money owed to you *prior to* your filing (such as, for example, tax refunds or commissions), but received *after,* may be taken by the trustee. Also, you should know that any life insurance proceeds (either because you are the beneficiary or because you have viaticated the policy) or any inheritance received by you within 180 days of your filing, or for a certain amount of time *after* your discharge, can potentially be taken by the bankruptcy trustee to pay off your creditors. Just be aware.

Life doesn't end with bankruptcy, and so you might ask yourself a practical question: "Can I keep my credit cards?" You probably cannot keep all of them, and it's just as well. After all, how did you get in this mess in the first place? Nevertheless, it is important that you keep at least one or two for car-rental purposes, convenience, etc. The problem is that many credit card companies (but not all) will automatically cancel the card upon being notified of the bankruptcy. The solution? Make sure the card(s) you want to keep are paid in full at the time you file. If they are, you are not required to list them as creditors, and you can keep those cards.

Be aware, though, that the trustee has the power to set aside unequal or "preferential" payments to creditors within the ninety days prior to filing, and certain other prior transfers as well. Do yourself a favor: think ahead, get a good lawyer (this may be the smartest money you ever spend!), and don't go into this blind.

15

Selling Your Life Insurance

Should you sell a life insurance policy? That's a good question, but not necessarily a simple one. That decision can be one of the best decisions you ever make or can open a Pandora's box of nightmarish proportions. Let's take a look at some of the issues involved.

In simple terms, the business (often referred to as the viatical settlement business) works like this:

Investors offer to pay you, in cash, a percentage of the face value of a policy. The amount you are offered is based on their best bet as to how long you have to live. The nearer to death they think you are, the greater the percentage you are offered and the more money you are paid. In return, you irrevocably assign to them ownership of the policy. When you die, they receive the full proceeds of the policy, thus receiving the return on their investment. At least in the past, that return has been substantial when compared with other, more orthodox investments. Thus, the business has expanded exponentially.

A growing number of people infected by HIV have sold their policies and find themselves with cash, ranging from tens to hundreds of thousands of dollars. Already, the transactions have had a dramatic impact on the community of people affected by HIV. In our law practice, we are dealing with an entirely new (and growing) group of clients: people who, in addition to dealing with health issues, for the first time in their lives find themselves with a sizable sum of cash and therefore need estate planning, advice on keeping their Medicaid or social security benefits, or other advice in dealing with their new situation.

Although the industry is definitely nontraditional, it is meeting a real need, and consumer demand for the service continues to swell. The financial pressures of living with HIV are obvious. It is also obvious, if you think about it, that a potential exists for real abuse by unscrupulous policy purchasers. It can be too easy to rip off people who are sick, living under severe financial pressures, and are desperate to get that cash in hand. Also, the business is still completely unregulated in many states, although the 1996 legislation we'll explore later in this chapter should provide a major push toward regulation. A growing number of states are already moving in that direction, however, so check with your state's insurance commissioner if you want to know for sure where you stand.

While most people in the business are fair dealers, and some of them are genuinely and deeply dedicated to the best interests of the AIDS community, a few can only be called scumbags. Please realize that the sale of your policy is extremely important to you. Too often, sellers view funds from a viatication as "found money" and don't bother to learn some essential basics of the industry, or even to push to get the highest bid possible. Take a moment and realize that, once that policy is gone, it's not coming back. In many cases, it may be your last real shot at achieving financial independence. Don't throw it away.

You should let an attorney or experienced financial adviser guide you through the process (if money is tight, ask them whether they would be willing to accept payment of their fee once you have received the proceeds), and possibly discuss the matter with an accountant. Make sure you've got yourself covered from the tax angle.

An Important Note on Current Developments

Recent treatment breakthroughs, especially the advent of drug "cocktails" including protease inhibitors, have at least temporarily cast the industry into disarray. Since the business is driven by investment decisions based on the anticipated life expectancy of the "viators," or people selling their policies, and no one currently has a clue as to the long-term effectiveness of the new treatments, the industry is in a wild state of flux.

As of this writing, some of the more conservative companies have temporarily stopped purchasing policies. Others have limited their interest to viators in advanced stages of the disease, while others are making lower offers. Since the industry is in such flux, if your health makes you eligible to viaticate, it is especially important that you understand how the industry works and use competitive bidding to your best advantage.

Before we take a closer look at the whole process, let's start off with an important point. *If you are HIV-positive, a life insurance policy can be a superb asset—almost like money in the bank!*

So don't let any policies you may have in force lapse. If you leave your job or are forced to retire because of disability, you may be able to convert your policy to keep it in force or to otherwise remain part of the employer's group. Do your homework to avoid throwing away an important asset.

Although it can be tough to keep making premium payments on a life insurance policy, think seriously about what a great asset the policy might be if you ever really need it, and be creative. Consider the following example:

> Craig leaves his job and finds himself unable to make premium payments on his life insurance policy. Instead of let-

ting the policy go, he works out a deal with his brother, which they put in writing, that his brother will pay the premiums. In return, Craig agrees to give his brother 135 percent of what he has paid, either when the policy is sold or when Craig dies.

The possibilities are endless. If you have life insurance coverage in place, think twice before letting it go.

"Accelerated Benefits" and You

Before you sell your policy, research whether your insurer offers an "accelerated benefits" option. A growing number of insurance companies, seeking to get in on the action begun by viatical settlement companies, are beginning to make such a feature available. If your company does offer this feature, and if you meet their strict health guidelines (i.e., very short life expectancy), you can receive a portion of the face value of your policy *directly from the insurance company*, at much more favorable rates than you would get from a "third-party," viatical settlement company. Also, unlike in viatications, the balance of the policy (subject to some charges) will remain available for your beneficiary. As a further benefit, you can often either viaticate the remainder of the policy, or leave that coverage in place for your beneficiary. Here is an example:

> Frank has a $100,000 policy with the Mutual Life Insurance Company, and his policy contains an accelerated-benefits rider. The company explains to him that, if his doctor certifies his life expectancy as six months or less, he can receive up to 50 percent of the face value of his policy. The amount given to Frank is treated by the company as (sort of) a loan, on which reasonable interest is charged and set off against the remaining half of the policy. As a re-

sult, some of the proceeds will remain available for Frank's beneficiary after his death.

Alternatively, Frank can then viaticate the balance of the policy (i.e., sell it to a viatical settlement company), receiving a much higher percentage on the overall transaction than if he had simply viaticated the whole policy. Let's say, for example, that Frank had sold the whole policy to a viatical company for 75 percent of its face value. He would have netted $75,000. By using the "blended" method, however, he receives $50,000 as accelerated benefits, then an additional $37,500 (75 percent of $50,000), totaling $87,500. That amounts to a difference of $12,500. Not bad, if you can get it!

Important note: Under the Health Insurance Portability and Accountability Act of 1996, the proceeds of qualified accelerated-benefits transactions are not federally taxable as income.

In summary, before you choose to viaticate, ask your insurance company the following questions:

1. Do you offer an "accelerated benefits" or "living benefits" option?
2. What is the maximum life expectancy I could have to qualify?
3. What percentage of the policy could I receive? Also, would I be prohibited from viaticating the balance of the policy?

Note: You should be aware that some unscrupulous purchasers have bought policies from unsuspecting sellers without disclosing to the sellers that the policies offer an accelerated benefits option. Then, after the deal has been completed, the new owners of the policies have exercised these options, making a windfall.

That is not a fair business practice. Don't let it happen to you.

THINKING ABOUT SELLING?

Should you sell your policy? Here are some of the issues you might need to think about:

1. Do you really need the money *now?* Even if your health might allow you to sell your policy now for a percentage of its face value, and even though it might really feel good to get the money, think long and hard before you make that choice. Realize that (unless you have more than one policy) your sale may be a one-shot deal. Think about whether you might really need that money in the future. And if you do sell, use your money wisely. It's all right to have a good time, just don't throw it away without thinking.

   A related point: If the size of your policy permits, think about selling only part of the policy. Some viatical settlement companies will buy your policy for a lesser amount of money and allow you to name a beneficiary on part of the policy. In essence, they are contracting to pay a portion of the policy benefits to your chosen beneficiary. If you are thinking along those lines, do your best to know the company you are doing business with; you are trusting them to act honorably after you have died.

2. Think about selling the policy to family members. Although such a transaction can raise weird issues, discuss frankly with your loved ones that a company of "strangers" stands to make a huge profit on the policy, and that you would rather keep it in the family. If you are able to work out a deal with loved ones, you might get a higher percentage, and you might also have more flexibility in structuring the transaction. Setting up the transaction as a "loan," for example, would avoid possible tax liabilities if you are unable to qualify for federal nontaxability.

3. Are you currently receiving any "means-based" benefits, such as Medicaid, food stamps, AFDC, etc.? If so, realize that receiving a sum of cash might (if the government finds out) make you ineligible for continued benefits. Selling your policy will not affect any health insurance policy you may have in place, nor will it affect any social security disability (SSD) payments you are receiving. However, it would terminate your right to receive supplemental security income (SSI), because those benefits are based on poverty.

   Most importantly, think seriously before you risk losing your Medicaid health insurance coverage. (Medicaid coverage is linked to your entitlement to SSI benefits.) If you are forced to pay for your own treatment, prescriptions, etc., your money is not going to last long, no matter how much you have gotten for your policy.
4. Are any of your beneficiaries really depending on you to provide for them after you are gone? Although you come first, just think it through before you decide to sell.
5. If you are thinking about viaticating a group policy issued as an employment benefit, consider the possibility that your doing so may alert your employer to your HIV status. One of the first steps to be taken by any viatical company with which you apply will be to *verify coverage* on the policy, which sometimes cannot be done without contacting your employer's benefits department. If this is a concern to you, discuss it carefully with the viatical companies with which you are applying. Find out exactly whom they will be approaching for information.

ONCE YOU DECIDE TO SELL

If you plan to deal with a viatical settlement company, you *must* take the time to understand the type of companies that are out there.

You have two basic choices: either you can deal with a *principal* or self-funded company, or you can work with a *broker* company. The former buys your policy from you directly, while the latter serves as a middleman, connecting you with a purchaser for your policy. To tell which kind of company you are dealing with, you need to ask. (It is usually not advertised.) As a general rule of thumb, if you are dealing with a broker, the policy will be assigned to a different corporate entity after the purchase is completed, although that is sometimes the case with "principal" company purchasers as well.

Understand that brokers do not work for free; they receive a commission for their services varying from 4 to 7 percent of the face value of the policy. Although they explain that their commission does not reduce your share, but instead "comes out of the purchaser's overhead," it is fair to question the validity of that statement. There is only so much of the pie to be cut, and that percentage of the face value's going to someone other than you might very well reduce the amount actually received by you.

A couple of other potential issues are raised in using a broker. If the commission is based on face value rather than the amount received by you, does the broker have an incentive to get you the highest deal possible? Might not the broker be guiding you toward a company that pays the highest commission rather than one that pays you the most money? Not necessarily, but it is a question worth asking.

You also need to make sure that a broker is genuinely shopping your policy around, as it claims to be, rather than taking the policy to only one possible purchaser. In some cases, companies have lied, making up one or two lower phantom offers to make the one actual bid they have seem better than it is. To get the highest offer, you need real competition, not just its appearance.

Please understand, our intention is *not* to make you paranoid about brokers. There is absolutely nothing wrong or second class about dealing with a broker rather than a principal company. In fact, many fine and committed people who helped start this business operate as brokers. The fact that a company is self-funded and not a broker offers no guarantee that they are honorable or fair dealers.

Also, in concept, dealing with a broker can simplify the procedure, as they verify your medical and insurance information, then take that information to competing purchasers for bids. Thus, the companies that may be interested in your policy do not need to independently obtain copies of your medical records and your insurance information. (Doctors and their staffs have sometimes become irritated when they have had to complete several questionnaires and make several copies of your medical records. At a minimum, let your doctor know what you are doing and how many companies you are applying with and make sure that will not be a problem.)

We mention these points only so that you will know the right questions to ask and increase the odds on maximizing the return on your policy. Before you sign any contracts, *always* try and get at least three to five bids. Further, if you need guidance in selecting a company or information about the industry in general, your best bet is to contact the Viatical Association of America, (800) 842-9811. The VAA represents the ethical leaders in the field and can be a valuable source for reliable information.

Finally, think about asking each company you choose to deal with the following questions:

1. Are you a self-funded or a broker company? Who will ultimately be the owner of my policy?
2. If you are dealing with a broker, ask the following questions: to which purchasing companies will you be taking my policy? Why? What is the percentage of your commission, and what will it be on my policy? Is that figure negotiable? Will you give me bids in writing from the different companies?
3. How will my confidentiality be protected? Who will be shown my application and/or medical records during the viatication

process? After the policy is sold, how will my privacy be protected?
4. Will you agree to have the funds put in escrow with an independent third party, and to confirm that you have done so in writing, at the same time or before I turn over the completed documents assigning ownership of the policy? The single best way to protect yourself in a viatical transaction is to require the use of an independent escrow agent. Typically, reputable companies have you sign a contract under which they agree to put your money in escrow as soon as they receive back from you the signed documents. While that is better than nothing, the better course is to request that the funds be put in escrow *before* you deliver the papers to them. Otherwise it may be difficult, practically speaking, to undo the transaction if the purchaser tries to scam you.
5. Is your company operating in the states where the industry is regulated? Have you applied for a license in New York, Florida, or California? If not, why not? How do you feel about regulation of the industry in general? The merits of regulation of the viatical settlement industry are now being vigorously debated. Some feel strongly that regulation is necessary to protect consumers who are often ill, desperate for cash, or both. They point out that the "high-risk, high-profits" viatical industry has attracted a wide variety of shady characters.

On the other hand, some argue that regulation will only interfere with the free market, ultimately drying up the number of investors needed to make the business flourish. They argue that regulation would be fine for the huge, funded companies, but might put the little guys out of business, weakening the competition that drives the bidding process and thus ultimately lessening the money received by viators.

While ethical and reasonable people stand firmly on both sides of the regulation debate, it is generally a positive sign if the company you are dealing with supports regulation. There have been abuses in the industry in the past, and until safeguards are put in place, they will reoccur. If someone is against regulation, that does not necessarily mean that he or she is slimy or a shady dealer, or even unethical. However, such unethical people, almost to a person, have taken a hard line against regulation. They don't want anyone looking at their history, setting standards for them, or otherwise interfering with the industry.

Just keep your eyes open as you deal in this business.

How Does It Work?

You start by filling out an application with the company you have chosen, which asks detailed questions about your health. At the same time, you authorize your doctor to release your entire medical records and to provide an opinion as to your life expectancy. Finally, you authorize your life insurance company to release full information about your policy, such as its value, the current beneficiaries, and whether it can be absolutely assigned.

Most policies, whether group or individual, can be assigned. Problems can arise, however, if the policy is less than two years old (the "contestability" period), because the company buying your policy may not be willing to risk that you might have misrepresented facts, etc., in the application. It can also be tricky if you are still in a "suicide exclusions" period, meaning that the insurer will not have to pay if you turn around and commit suicide tomorrow. Viatical companies are not willing to assume that risk either. Otherwise, your policy is probably eligible to be sold.

Health Analysis from a Viatical Perspective

The company buying your insurance is basing their investment on their assessment of your life expectancy. Obviously, they do not know when you are going to die and are estimating based upon statistics. So don't get superstitious and assume that they know something that you don't! Also, their independent physicians review your records and evaluate that question. They factor in an assumption that your personal physician is likely to protect you by taking the most dim view possible of your life expectancy. Don't worry about the medical assessment phase, though, because you cannot do much about it. The only important step you can take is to make sure, on an ongoing basis, that your medical records reflect any problems you have experienced as a result of HIV.

Based upon your health profile you are offered a percentage of the face value of the policy. How much of a percentage is a good deal? That depends totally on your situation. Generally, the percentage should not be less than half, unless unusual circumstances apply. As of now, the market is in a total state of flux and new standards are emerging. The companies base their offers upon such information as your T-cell count, and specifically whether you have experienced one or more serious opportunistic infections. In a sense, the worse off your health *appears* to be on paper, the better off you will be in this transaction.

Before you accept an offer, ask around (whether friends who have sold their policies or AIDS services organizations near you) to see if the offer that has been made to you is in line. Keep in mind, however, that yesterday's percentages may no longer apply. The significant treatment advances that have arisen for HIV may mean bad news for the viatical industry, and for those selling their policies. Do not make the mistake of treating such an important decision casually. It is now more important than ever to make the very best deal possible for yourself.

A Word to the Wise

Always keep in mind that no matter how nice the people you are dealing with might seem to be, their interests may not be the same as yours. Often, in fact, their goals may directly clash with yours. You want to maximize the percentage paid out to you, whereas they may want the opposite. Beware of companies using high-pressure tactics (such as "this offer will remain open for only twenty-four hours," because that is *never* true), companies that request that you apply only with them, or that pressure you to sell more than one of your policies even if you are not so inclined. Remember, you are in the driver's seat.

Also, do not rely on verbal promises, no matter how nice or charming the people seem, and take pains to make sure your backside is covered. It's better to be careful during the process than to live with regret in the months and years that follow.

ARE YOUR PROCEEDS TAXABLE AS INCOME?

The answer to this important question is changing. Historically, since the relatively recent development of the viatical settlement industry, the answer has been yes. Even though generally the proceeds of life insurance policies paid out by reason of your death are not taxable as income to the *beneficiary*, i.e., in the typical situation in which the funds are paid out after your death, the proceeds have been taxable to *you* if you viaticate the policy during your lifetime. Since the viatical companies have not been required to report the payments to the IRS, however, many viators have chosen to play "audit roulette" and not declare the income.

In the past, many viators dealing with serious HIV illness made this decision lightly, reasoning that "by the time the IRS catches up with me, I won't be around anyway." With the current state of HIV treatment, such thinking can be extremely dangerous. Improved medicines, drug combinations, and better therapies might keep you alive longer than you might have thought. In at least a few cases, the IRS has caught up with viators who chose not to report the income, and assessed taxes and penalties.

The good news is that, if you handle your viatical transaction carefully, the proceeds should be officially nontaxable. To understand how, let's take a look at the recent federal legislation known as the Health Insurance Portability and Accountability Act of 1996. The law amends the federal tax law to exempt the proceeds of viatical settlements from taxation *under certain circumstances*. Under the law, three factors must simultaneously occur for the funds you receive to be nontaxable. You must be a *terminally ill individual*, the company you are dealing with must be a *viatical settlement provider*, and the funds must be received by you after *December 31, 1996* (no matter what the date you entered into the contract). If your situation does not fit each of the above criteria, the proceeds will still remain taxable.

Let's look at how the legislation defines some important terms:
Terminally ill individual. From a tax perspective, this is how you want to be defined. Under the law, you fall within this category if you have "been certified by a physician as having an illness or physical condition which can reasonably be expected to result in death in twenty-four months or less after the date of the certification." You are home free in terms of taxability if *any* physician (it need not necessarily be *your* physician) is willing to sign such a certification on your behalf. Although the law specifies no requirement that the certifying physician be *your* physician, that may be instituted through future regulations. Check with a viatical company or the VAA on this point before you sell.

The physician is not certifying that you *will* die within that time, just that a reasonable possibility exists of that outcome. Put this in perspective: the IRS is in a poor position to second-guess medical opinions, and you can probably decide with comfort not to report the proceeds so long as you have the certification in your file and the company is a "provider" as defined in the law (we will explain that below).

With the advent of protease inhibitors and other new treatments, however, it may be more difficult to fit within this category than the drafters of the legislation probably originally intended. That will only become clear over time. Nevertheless, if you are aiming for nontaxability, it is essential that you do fit in.

Chronically ill individual. If you are unable to obtain certification as "terminally ill," things get considerably more murky, and the law will probably offer you no relief from taxation. The law also exempts from taxation, under certain circumstances, insurance proceeds received by people classified as "chronically ill." Unlike the category of "terminal illness," defined by a relatively simple reference to life expectancy, "chronic illness" requires certification that you are unable to meet at least two of the basic activities of daily living (such as eating, bathing and dressing yourself, using the toilet, etc.) without assistance for ninety days. You will not fit within this category unless you require a nursing-home level of care, and you will certainly not qualify if you are asymptomatic with HIV infection.

This section of the law will be of limited usefulness to people with HIV. If you require nursing home care, you should be able to obtain certification as "terminally ill," thus avoiding this complicated issue. Further, under the law, the viatical proceeds received by the "chronically ill" are apparently exempt from taxation only if they are used to pay the costs of "qualified long-term care services," basically nursing home care. Finally, the legislation requires that complete information on such payouts, including your name, address, and social security number, be reported to the IRS by the viatical company.

It is widely anticipated that regulations will be issued by the U.S. Treasury Department imposing similar reporting requirements for viators in that category, and possibly all viators. (Those regulations may be in place by the time you decide to viaticate your policy. At that point, ask the companies you are dealing with whether they will be required to report the transaction to the IRS.) Keep in mind, though, that so long as you have been certified as "terminally ill" and are dealing with a qualified "provider" (see below) you should not be concerned about reporting, since the proceeds will not be taxable.

Viatical settlement providers. Even if you are certified as terminally ill, you must still deal with a company that is a qualified "provider" as defined under the law to ensure that your proceeds will be tax-free. To qualify, the company must be "regularly engaged" in the business, *and* either (1) licensed to do business in your state, *or* (2) meet other standards as defined in the law. Let's take a closer look at these two categories.

1. *Licensing.* First, understand that the company must be licensed only if you live in a state that has passed legislation requiring the licensing of viatical companies. To find out whether your state falls within that category, ask the viatical companies you are dealing with, and call the office of your state's insurance commissioner to check on the current status of the law. Since a growing number of states are passing laws regulating the industry and requiring licensing, it is important that you check for current information.

   If your state does not require licensing, move to section (2) below. If it does, ask the above sources whether the companies in question have been licensed, or whether they have applied for licensure. Even if they have not yet been granted a license, but have applications pending, you will probably still be protected since the companies are operating in accordance with state licensing requirements. If the company is licensed or its application is pending in your state, you are dealing with a qualified *viatical settlement provider* and your inquiry can stop there. If not, seriously consider taking your business elsewhere. Even if such a company is offering a higher percentage, the offer probably does not stack up when taxation is figured into the picture.

2. *If your state does not require licensing.* Although the long-term effect of the federal legislation will almost certainly be to drive more states to require licensing of the viatical industry, many states still have no such requirement. If that is the case where you live, to qualify as a *provider* under the law, the company must meet the requirements of sections 8 and 9 of the Viatical Settlements Model Act (the Act) as promulgated by the National Association of Insurance Commissioners, as well as the standards set forth in section 4 of the Viatical Settlement Model Regulations (the Regulations), titled "Standards for Evaluation of Reasonable Payments." Since the burden falls on you to verify the company's status if you want to successfully avoid the imposition of taxes, pay careful attention to the following requirements. In order to protect yourself, make sure that they are all followed to the letter.

Section 8 of the Act. Requires that the company disclose the following information to you *no later than* the date the contract is signed for the deal. This information is typically provided on one disclosure form:
   a. Possible alternatives to viatication, including accelerated benefits offered by the insurer.
   b. The possible taxability of the proceeds.
   c. That the proceeds could be subject to the claims of creditors.
   d. The possible adverse effect on your eligibility for Medicaid and/or other means-based benefits.
   e. Your right to cancel the deal within thirty days of the signing of the contract or fifteen days after you have received the money, whichever is less.
   f. The date you will get your money, and from whom.

Section 9 of the Act. Establishes certain rules for viatical companies, as follows:

a. Before entering into the contract, the company must first obtain (1) a written statement from your doctor that you are of sound mind and under no constraint or undue influence, and (2) a witnessed document in which you *consent to the viatical settlement contract, acknowledge that you have a "catastrophic or life-threatening disease," acknowledge your complete understanding of the contract and of the benefits available under the policy, release your medical records, and acknowledge that you have entered into the transaction freely and voluntarily.*
b. All medical information requested by the company must be handled in accordance with state laws on confidentiality.
c. All contracts must allow you to unconditionally cancel the contract and refund the money at least thirty days from the date of the contract or fifteen days after you have received the money, whichever is less.
d. Immediately after receiving the signed contract and documents assigning ownership of the policy, the company is required to pay the proceeds of the settlement into an independently operated escrow account, until confirmation of the assignment is provided to the company by the insurance company. Immediately following such confirmation, the funds must be released to you, the viator. This is a key step, both for your protection in the transaction and to ensure nontaxability.
e. Failure to deliver the funds to you by the promised date (see the last requirement in section 8, above) renders the contract null and void.

Section 4 of the Regulations. Titled "Standards for Evaluation of Reasonable Payments," this schedule is intended to establish a rough uniformity for the industry between the viator's estimated life expectancy and the amount of the payout, and to provide a degree of consumer protection to ignorant (and/or desperate) consumers. Calculated long before the advent of the recent, more effective treatments, those minimum rates are as follows:

INSURED'S LIFE EXPECTANCY	MINIMUM PERCENTAGE OF FACE VALUE
Less than 6 months	80
At least 6 but less than 12 months	70
At least 12 but less than 18 months	65
At least 18 but less than 24 months	60
24 months or more	50

If medical advances continue, the above percentages could very well drop. In the meantime, the law probably *does not* require exact compliance by the company with the above schedule in every deal. To make sure that you are dealing with a qualified provider, check out carefully their compliance with the above standards. Do not hesitate to bring to their attention any area in which they might be falling short.

On some of the requirements, however, it may be difficult or impossible for you to know what the company is doing in other cases. Make sure that the company has strictly followed the above rules. To best protect yourself, also request that the company warrant through a written certification that it "meets the requirements of sections 8 and 9 of the Viatical Settlements Model Act of the National Association of Insurance Commissioners, and meets the requirements of the Model Regulations of the National Association of Insurance Commissioners (relating to standards for evaluation of reasonable payments) in determining amounts paid in its viatical transactions." This language tracks the law, and such a certification should help give you peace of mind if you are unsure about whether the company meets any of the above requirements.

You'll be fine, but you do need to understand how the tax provisions work, and to do your best to meet the law's requirements for nontaxability.

Never forget that the burden remains on you to protect yourself. Even though states are increasingly moving in the direction of regulation, some questionable companies are still doing business out there, and you need to keep your eyes wide open.

Let's look at an example of what can happen if things go bad:

> In the years following his HIV diagnosis, James lost his good health, his ability to work, his job, and eventually his health insurance benefits. With financial pressures beginning to mount, he found it increasingly difficult even to pay the premiums on the one life insurance policy he had been able to keep. Thumbing through a gay magazine one week, he noticed an ad for a viatical settlement company called Great Northern Viatical Corporation. The ad sure looked good, with the company promising a "7 day guarantee" on the approval process, no middlemen involved, and $25 million in the bank set aside to help the terminally ill by buying their policies. Besides, he had seen their ads in a handful of other magazines and figured they must be doing all right.
>
> On June 8, 1993, James signed an agreement with the company irrevocably assigning his $100,000 policy to the company in return for its promise to immediately pay him $50,000 in cash. By the end of the month, he still hadn't received the money, only a letter promising payment "on or

before July 12, 1993." By now, James had long since started to get nervous. But his troubles (and stress) were only beginning, and he heard nothing from the company until he received a letter dated August 18, 1993.

That letter spoke of "an unexpected delay," offered an unintelligible explanation, and enclosed a small check as "an option extension retainer" to string James along. According to the letter, the "latest date possible for actual disbursement is September 7, 1993," nearly three months after payment was to have been made. On September 9, James was mailed a letter promising payment "no later than October 6, 1993." To add supreme insult to injury, the letter stated that "if your policy should mature prior to your receiving full disbursement, proceeds . . . will be disbursed to your estate." In other words, the company, having successfully delayed payment of its obligations for months, planned to take its cut of the policy whether or not James ever saw the money he was promised during his lifetime.

That is about as low, and as outrageous, as it gets. Even though James ultimately recovered his money, no one can gauge or compensate him for the harm caused by the stress of being ripped off while he was down. Just don't let it happen to you.

16

Discrimination: What Are Your Rights?

We live in a society in which people with HIV are often treated like lepers and deprived of an opportunity to keep earning a living even though they are (in many cases) well able to keep working. We live in a society in which HIV is sometimes seen to be "God's judgment," where the branding of the buttocks of HIV-positive people has been seriously discussed, and where quarantine has been vigorously debated as a means of dealing with the threat to public health presented by AIDS.

Already, a multitude of lawsuits based on claims of HIV-related discrimination have been brought in state and federal courts across the land, and the end is nowhere in sight. We have seen only the tip of the iceberg of the epidemic, and employers, ignorant of the law, continue to illegally discriminate against HIV-positive employees. As noted in the law, "Society's myths and fears about disability and disease are as handicapping as are the physical limitations that flow from actual impairments." To protect yourself, it is more important than ever that you know your rights.

First, let's consider the following real-life scenarios:

> A waiter employed by a private club confides in his supervisor about his HIV status and within weeks gets a telephone call from the club manager, telling him not to come back to work "because this kind of thing would obviously not be acceptable to the members." The waiter is out of a job.

A young man agrees to "come out" and be interviewed as HIV-positive on a Spanish-language TV show. He returns to his apartment only to find that all of his possessions have been placed out on the street.

Out of the blue, an HIV-positive woman working as a secretary is fired based on "a decline in her job performance." She knows that the claim is untrue, and ultimately proves in court that her employers learned of her HIV status through her insurance claims and fired her in an effort to keep the company's group health insurance premiums reasonable.

A man acting as a caretaker to his lover, who is sick with AIDS, is fired from his job. Although the company apparently assumes their employee is HIV-positive and cannot allow "that type of person" to stay on, he is in fact HIV-negative. Nevertheless, the employee still prevails in a lawsuit challenging the firing as discriminatory, because he was *believed* to be HIV-positive and is legally protected on that basis.

HIV infection is treated as a "handicap" under both state and federal law, and that is the basis of your protection.

The word *handicap* makes many of us think of such obvious examples as the need for a wheelchair, blindness, or deafness. But the term is much broader than that, defined as any "physical or mental impairment" that "substantially limits one or more . . . major life activities." The scope of the law is intentionally broad, designed to protect all groups working at a disadvantage and to provide them with equal opportunities.

Why would a person with HIV, but who is completely healthy, also be protected as "handicapped" under the law? The reason is simple: in light of the fear and hysteria out there, simply having the virus is enough to turn you into an outcast, cut off against your will from any means of supporting yourself, and subject to the loss of housing and other basic rights. Even if you are HIV-negative but are mistakenly believed to be positive, you also need protection.

Focus on the "Americans with Disabilities" Act

If you are living with HIV, it is essential that you be familiar with at least the basics of the federal Americans with Disabilities Act, commonly referred to as the ADA. Although you are probably also protected under state law from such discrimination, those laws vary across the country. Do not ignore any such rights; take the time to find out how the laws of your state might protect you, and how you can put them to work for you.

In the meantime, though, let's look at the ADA, an important federal law that safeguards your rights no matter where you live in the United States. Since its passage in 1990, the law has dramatically redefined discrimination law and continues to do so with each new court battle being pursued. Let's look at the basics of the law.

First, if you have HIV (or are believed to) and work for an employer of at least fifteen people (including also state and local governments, labor unions, etc.), you are protected from employment discrimination under the ADA. The law offers strong legal protections at virtually every stage of employment, including in application and hiring as well as promotions and benefits.

Although this book will focus on employment issues, you should also know that the ADA protects you from discrimination in public accommodations (which includes restaurants, stores, and virtually every other service you might use as a consumer), transportation, and public services. In each case, it is against the law for you to receive different or worse treatment because you are either HIV-positive or believed to be.

Now, back to employment. The law protects you if you are a

qualified employee, meaning that you are able to "meet the essential requirements of the job." Please understand that the law does *not* guarantee you job security because you are positive or have AIDS. First, you must physically be able to do the job, whatever that requires. Second, you can be fired or laid off just like any other worker, but you cannot be fired or let go *because* of your HIV status. As you can imagine, some lively debates take place in court as to the employer's motivation behind the action in question.

Sometimes people with HIV can do their jobs, but need a little flexibility from their employers. For example, people may need time off for naps, visits to the doctor, etc., may need to work part-time, or need other arrangements to keep working.

Under such circumstances, the ADA requires employers to make a *reasonable accommodation* to the employee, if necessary. What is *reasonable*? That depends on a number of factors, including the nature of the job, the size of the company, etc. Some examples mentioned in the law include

- restructuring the job after taking into consideration any limitations (physical or mental) resulting from the disability.
- establishing a part-time or modified work schedule.
- assigning the employee to a vacant position, where more flexibility may be possible.

If changes such as these will allow you to keep doing your job despite the changes resulting from HIV, you have the legal right to request them if your company is covered by the ADA. If it is not, it is especially important that you learn about your rights under state law.

The law does not require the employer to make a requested accommodation to your disability if it would impose an *undue hardship* on the operation of the business. What does that mean? It depends on the specifics of your situation. These are only the barebones legal terms, with no simple definition in every case.

In deciding whether a proposed accommodation would impose an undue hardship, a court takes into consideration the cost to the company, its financial resources, and the number of employees. Generally, the larger and wealthier the company, the more flexibility will be required by the courts in structuring an arrangement that will allow the employee to keep working.

It all comes down to a balancing act between your rights and the employer's, and depends on the facts of each situation. You will probably need to consult a lawyer if it comes down to an argument over this point, because the law is tricky in this area. This is the bottom line: if you are able to do the job, without or *with* a reasonable accommodation, you have the legal right to get the job or to keep on working if you already have it.

WHAT EMPLOYERS CAN AND CANNOT DO

The ADA distinguishes between actions that can be taken by an employer, or questions that may be asked, at different stages of employment. The law distinguishes between the following phases of that process: (1) *preemployment, pre-offer,* (2) *preemployment, postoffer,* and (3) *postemployment.* Generally speaking, employers are extremely limited during the first phase, so people with disabilities can get their foot in the door.

The second phase is substantially more open (but important restrictions still apply), and the employer's latitude is once again extremely limited during the third phase. To explain, let's take a look at an example:

> Roberta is fed up with her job working in a fast-food restaurant and has been for the last couple of years. Nevertheless, she has hesitated to make a change because of her HIV status. Although she is in generally good health, she has been positive for ten years and was hospitalized last year

with PCP. She sees her doctor every few months and is currently taking an HIV drug combination. She only rarely misses work.

After doing her homework, she decides to look for a job as a legal secretary. In response to a classified ad, she calls and sets up an interview with the managing partner of the law firm of Sacco & Vanzetti (the Firm).

1. **Preemployment, pre-offer.** At this stage, the Firm is extremely limited in the questions it can ask about any disability Roberta might have. It *can* ask her about her ability to meet the specific requirements of being a secretary, such as her experience, etc. It *cannot* ask whether she has any disabilities, or about the nature and severity of any disabilities that may be obvious. (For example, if Roberta has KS lesions on her hands or face, the Firm cannot inquire about that. If they do, Roberta is, practically speaking, in an extremely tough spot, but she has no legal duty to answer the question.)

   Similarly, the Firm *cannot* ask questions about Roberta's medical status during this phase. It would be illegal for the Firm to ask whether she has a medical condition, whether she is taking any prescription drugs, or whether she took many sick days from her prior job.

   Further, the Firm is legally prohibited from either asking these questions of Roberta's prior employer, hiring an investigative service to do so, or otherwise making efforts to get this information.

   The Firm *can* make a job offer to Roberta conditioned on the results of a *postoffer* medical exam or inquiry, but only if *all* candidates applying for that job category are required to do the same. If any such exam is conducted, any medical information received must be kept completely confidential by the Firm and kept in a place other than in Roberta's employee file. The exam cannot be discriminatory in its intent.

With the advent of drug testing in the workplace, new conflicts have arisen between employees' rights to privacy and the employers' rights to a "drug-free" workplace. The conflict has hit particularly hard some people with HIV, when employers get carried away with their testing programs and inquire about *legal* drug use, such as the prescription drugs you are taking for your HIV infection.

What if, for example, the Firm asked Roberta, "Are you taking any prescription drugs?" as part of a drug-testing program? That question would be illegal, because it obviously forces the disclosure of her HIV status. (Very few who are not HIV-positive are currently taking AZT!)

Nevertheless, even if the question is illegal, there it is, and to refuse to answer the question will certainly raise major red flags to the employer. What would I do? It's a tough call, but I would probably exercise my right to medical privacy about my HIV status and answer "None." Hopefully, that will end the matter.

This issue may arise less frequently in the future because guidelines now in place suggest that such inquiries, if they are to be made at all as part of a drug-testing program, be made only in the event a positive test for drug use has come back. If confronted with that, think about having your doctor simply certify that you are currently taking a prescription drug that might result in a positive test. The name of the drug need not be disclosed, although practically speaking the damage may have been done.

2. **Preemployment, postoffer.** Once Roberta has received a formal offer of employment, the Firm has considerable latitude in asking medical questions, performing tests, etc. The limitations set forth in the paragraph above all apply. The employer *cannot* do any tests on Roberta that it does not do on *everyone* applying for that job category, and it cannot use the results as a reason not to hire her unless there is a legitimate *business* rea-

son for doing so. Fear of HIV won't cut it as a reason to revoke an offer and not hire.

The law is set up this way in an effort to balance the competing rights of all parties involved. It protects job applicants by allowing for easy identification of discriminatory hiring practices, but also protects the employer by allowing the timely discovery of any condition that would legitimately bear on the ability of a prospective employee to do the job in question.

3. **Postemployment.** Once Roberta has been hired by the company, strict limits apply on any inquiries as to disabilities, physical exams, etc. Again, if any such actions are to be taken, a legitimate business reason must exist to take them.

A Note on Confidentiality

Although you may cringe at the idea of prospective employers holding information on your being HIV-positive or on your medical status, there is some consolation. The ADA makes any such information extremely confidential, defining it as "confidential medical record." According to the ADA, the information *cannot* be placed in your employment file, but must be kept in a separate, locked cabinet. Further, access to that cabinet must be limited to certain specifically designated personnel.

If you feel you've been discriminated against, *immediately* consult an attorney. A growing number of lawyers specialize in employment discrimination, and it is getting easier to find attorneys to represent you on HIV-related claims. It is not absolutely essential that attorneys have experience with HIV cases (although obviously that's preferred), but they should be familiar with employment discrimination cases.

It is important that you move on your case quickly, because if you do not, you may miss important deadlines that could leave your case dead in the water. Also, realize that if you sign a general release to the company at the time you leave, in return for a little extra pay or whatever, you will have given up all of your rights to pursue a lawsuit against them.

If you have been discriminated against because of HIV or been denied a reasonable accommodation that would allow you to keep on working, you must file a claim with the Equal Employment Opportunity Commission (EEOC) within three hundred days of the alleged discriminatory act to preserve your rights to sue under the ADA.

You should consult an attorney at this stage because often you will want to file both with the EEOC and with the appropriate agency in your state. This stage can be tricky; make sure you get some help. If you have a valid claim, it can be an extremely important asset. Make sure you take good care of it.

Once you have filed with the EEOC, they will investigate the charge and determine if "reasonable cause" exists to believe that discrimination has occurred. Once it has issued its finding, or earlier if requested by the claimant, the EEOC will issue a Notice of Right to Sue, after which you will have ninety days to file a private lawsuit in state or federal court.

As you probably know, the world of employment can be a jungle. If you find yourself lost out there, take the time to study the map offered by the ADA. It might lead you to safety!

17

A Survival Guide to HIV in the Workplace

Now we will take a close, practical look at things you need to think about with regard to your job if you have HIV. Too often, people navigating through the challenges of life with HIV find employment issues particularly sticky.

Nevertheless, there is good news for the HIV-positive. Not only is it illegal for your employer to fire you on that basis, but it is also illegal to demote you, deny you pay raises or bonuses, or otherwise treat you differently in any way (including benefits) than they do their other employees. The smarter your employer is, the quicker they'll realize that treating you differently because you're HIV-positive can get them into quick and serious trouble.

The protections of the law notwithstanding, people with HIV are still fired fairly often because of it. A frightening amount of fear and ignorance about the disease is still out there, and often once the word gets out, people with HIV risk either obvious or subtle harassment from bosses, coworkers, etc., and/or isolation on the job. Sometimes that can make doing your job impossible.

CONFIDENTIALITY

The first thing you need to realize is that your HIV status *is your own business!* Under the laws of most states, you have a complete right of privacy with regard to that information, and generally no employers have any right to know. Although it can be tempting to break the silence and ease the loneliness by telling a coworker what's going on, think twice before you take that step. Think about joining a support group or talking to friends not connected to the business before you share that information with people at work. Once spoken the words cannot be taken back, and you cannot control how far they will go.

FILING INSURANCE CLAIMS

Depending on the type of insurance plan your employer uses, they may receive notice that you are receiving treatment for HIV if certain medical bills are submitted to the plan for payment. (This is particularly tricky when the company's insurance plan is "self-funded," meaning that all claims are processed by "in house" employees.)

If you are concerned, think about speaking with the head of that department and putting that person on notice that HIV information is legally confidential. Yes, that's a bold move, but sometimes people need a little education.

Also, although getting the medical care you need has got to be your top priority, think about getting your blood work done privately if periodic monitoring is all you need at this point. Particularly if you have reason to fear your employer's reaction, it may be worth it to take this step. On the other hand, if you need more acute (and expensive) medical care, get it! Don't play games if your health can't afford it.

PROTECT YOURSELF!

Although the law gives you the right not to, you should at least think about formally notifying your employer about your HIV if you are fairly certain that they already know, and if you feel that you are being set up to be fired and need to protect yourself. Why? Because the first requirement in proving any case of HIV discrimination is establishing that the employer knew about the HIV before firing you. (Obviously, if they had no knowledge, they could not have discriminated against you on that basis. Legally speaking, discrimination is an action requiring intent.)

In the movie *Philadelphia*, a major issue (and difficulty) at trial was proving that the employer had known of Andrew Beckett's status when it fired him. Beckett's whole case hinged upon proving to the jury that one of his bosses had noticed a small KS lesion on his forehead and that he had made a connection to AIDS.

Had Beckett created a record of having informed his employers, such as by telling them in the presence of a witness, or through a certified letter, return receipt requested, the whole issue could have been avoided. Although the idea seems risky, telling your employer sends two messages: you are not afraid or ashamed of being positive, and you know your rights and are not willing to accept any harassment or abuse. The substance of such a letter could go something like this:

> Dear Employer:
>
> This letter shall serve to put you on notice that I have been diagnosed with HIV (or AIDS, whichever applies). At this time, I am fully able to meet the requirements of my job and look forward to many more years of service with the company. If you have any questions or concerns, please feel free to address them to my attorney, Jane Doe, Esq.
>
> Sincerely yours,
>
>
> cc: Jane Doe, Esq.

Also, telling your employer increases the possibility that your bosses will seek legal advice, which will probably be good for you.

Any good lawyer will tell his or her client that it's plain stupid to fire an employee because of HIV. The bottom line is this: it's better to have a job than a lawsuit, but you have got to take whatever action necessary to protect yourself.

Remember that the employer's duty to extend to you a reasonable accommodation does not commence until you have given notice that you need one. Accordingly, if you feel that your health has reached a point where something needs to change to allow you to keep working, think about letting your employer know what's going on. Don't be afraid, but do move cautiously and try to know your rights and have a plan in place before you leap.

What If You're Not Feeling So Hot?

Don't kill yourself working; neither the law nor common sense requires you to. If HIV has affected your ability to put in a good day's work, be aware that you may have the legal right to demand a reasonable accommodation.

For example, you may need a flexible schedule to arrange your medical visits, etc., or you may need time off because of fatigue. Such changes are your legal right. The law does not prevent your employer from firing you if you are no longer able to work; it only guarantees that you will be allowed to work as long as possible. Of course, if you work less, your employer is allowed to pay you less, but cannot legally alter your insurance benefits, etc.

Know Your Rights under the Family Medical Leave Act

If you are living and working with HIV, you should also be aware of the important rights available to you under the federal Family and Medical Leave Act of 1993. All employers of fifty or more employees are covered by this law, and you are eligible for its protections if at least that many employees work for your company within a seventy-five-mile radius. (This can be a problem if the company you work for is spread out over a large geographical area.)

Basically, the law forces such employers to allow employees to take up to twelve weeks of unpaid leave per year, if, among other reasons, the employee is needed to care for a "child, spouse or parent with a serious health condition," or if "the employee's own serious health condition makes the employee unable to do his or her job." Unfortunately, under the first option, gay caretakers, or unmarried straight couples, are out of luck because they are not legally spouses. The second option, however, can be extremely helpful.

To take advantage of the law, you must have been with the company at least a year and worked at least 1,250 hours during the last twelve months. If you are a "key employee," however, meaning that you are in the top-paid 10 percent of the employees of your company within a seventy-five-mile radius, and the employer follows certain notice requirements, you can be excluded from the benefits of the act. If you are that important to the company, however, you may be in a position to apply some leverage to get what you want.

Although unpaid leave may not sound that great, the beauty of the law is that employers are required to keep insurance coverage and other benefits in place, and to let the employees come back to a position at the same level, and benefits, as when they left. Think about it: if you have been sick but you feel that you are not ready to go on permanent disability, the FMLA may create a great opportunity for you to take a break and concentrate on healing. The security of knowing that you have the right to return to work can make a major difference for you.

As to your group health insurance coverage, if your employer typically pays your premiums for you, it must keep doing so while you are on leave. On the other hand, if you ordinarily contribute toward payment, that does not change. (The same applies to payment of spouse/dependent premiums.) The employer's obligation to keep your health benefits in force ends if (1) you fail to make any required payments within thirty days after they are due, (2) you announce that you will not be returning to work or just never show up, or (3) you use up all of your time for leave under this act. If your coverage ceases under this act, check out your rights to COBRA coverage (see chapter 11).

If you seek leave because of your own illness, you must provide medical certification that you cannot perform your regular duties. If the employer disagrees with you, it can ask for a second opinion. If their expert disagrees with yours, they choose a third expert together, whose opinion will be binding.

Further, especially if you are taking the time because of your own illness, you may take the time either in a "lump sum" or, interestingly, on a part-time or intermittent basis. Under the second option, only the time actually taken by you, whether it is one day or four hours a week, will count toward your twelve-week limit. If nothing else, the law provides you with authority to negotiate with your employer an arrangement that works for you.

Keep in mind that the FMLA is only a legal minimum, representing the basic requirements for employers of a certain size. In some cases, employers on good terms with their workers may go beyond the minimum requirements of the act. Find out your employer's policy (if there is one!) on these matters.

Finally, if you plan to exercise your rights under FMLA, the law requires you to provide notice to your employer at least thirty days prior to taking your leave, unless your situation was not "foreseeable." In the latter case, notice must be given "as soon as practicable." Take a careful look at the terms of FMLA before you need it.

TO WRAP IT UP

In summary, realize that you do have strong legal protections as a person living with HIV, and learn about your rights so you will not have to guess about them and live in fear or uncertainty.

An increasing number of lawsuits are being filed under the ADA and state law alleging HIV discrimination, and the end is nowhere in sight. As a result, it's not as hard as it used to be to find a lawyer to take your case, if it comes down to that. By knowing your rights, though, you can increase the odds of receiving your due without a lawsuit. That's the way it should be. Trust me: if you can possibly avoid it, you do not need the hassle. A job beats a lawsuit hands down!

Conclusion

In this book, we have only begun to scratch the surface of the legal issues raised by life with HIV. As you can see, a dizzying number of medical, legal, and psychological issues seem to necessarily follow an HIV diagnosis, and the merry-go-round trip through the system that follows. While this book probably will not answer your questions with specificity, we sincerely hope it may at least guide you through some of the more difficult issues and spare you a little bit of heartache. We hope that by recognizing an issue before it hits you over the head, you may be able to avoid it completely or at least minimize its impact.

Please do not be afraid or hesitant to take advantage of any source of information out there to help get you through, including legal assistance if called for. Asking for help is never anything to be ashamed of, and HIV presents challenges that it may be almost impossible to deal with alone. When it comes to HIV, it is indeed true that just because you may be paranoid does not mean they (insurers, employers, etc.) are not out to get you!

May we all live to one day look back on the AIDS crisis as an historical incident. Until that blessed day arrives, please do your best to protect yourself and those you love.

APPENDIX A: GLOSSARY OF TERMS

Accelerated benefits: A possible alternative to *viatication,* involving a deal with the company issuing your insurance policy instead of a third-party viatical company. If you meet strict life expectancy guidelines (typically one year or less) and if your insurance company offers such a benefit, you can receive a certain percentage of your policy now and most of the balance will remain available for your beneficiaries. Alternatively, you can sometimes *viaticate* the remaining balance on the policy to a viatical company, yielding you the highest immediate cash return from the policy. Also sometimes referred to as *living benefits* provisions.

Administrative hearing: In social security appeals, the level of review at which most reversals are obtained. At this stage, a hearing is conducted by an administrative law judge (ALJ) to determine whether the *DDS* was wrong in finding you not to be disabled.

Americans with Disabilities Act (ADA): A federal law passed in 1990 that prohibits employers of at least fifteen people from discriminating against people with disabilities (including HIV). Also prevents discrimination with respect to public accommodations, including restaurants, stores, public transportation, etc. Requires employers to make *reasonable accommodations,* if necessary, to allow people with disabilities to keep working.

Bankruptcy: A federal court procedure intended to give debtors a fresh start by eliminating some of their debt. Although different procedures are available, the most popular type of individual bankruptcy is Chapter 7, or liquidation.

Capitation: In managed care, a payment mechanism through which *HMOs* and *PPOs* pay their participating doctors a fixed amount per patient per month, often without regard to the specific health status of the individual patient.

COBRA: A federal law requiring employers of at least twenty people to offer to keep in force group health insurance coverage for at least eighteen months for people who have left their jobs or who would otherwise no longer qualify to remain covered as part of the group. (People who leave their jobs as a result of disability may be entitled to twenty-nine months, and others losing their coverage as dependents thirty-six months.) During the time coverage is extended, it remains the responsibility of the covered individual to make his or her own premium payments. Some states have adopted *Mini-COBRA laws,* requiring companies of fewer than twenty to provide similar benefits.

Conversion: A right to switch coverage extended as part of a group, often health or life insurance, to an individual policy upon leaving your employment without *evidence of insurability.*

Coordination of benefits: Typically found in disability and health policies, provisions that reduce benefits payable under the policy by governmental (such as Social Security or Medicare) or other benefits you may be receiving.

Creditable coverage: Under health insurance reform legislation, prior health insurance coverage of virtually any kind, including *Medicare* or *Medicaid,* for which credit is given month for month to reduce any applicable exclusion periods for *preexisting conditions* in new coverage. Such credit is given for the prior coverage only if no gap lasting sixty-three days or more has occurred between the old coverage and the new.

Disability Determination Services (DDS): Agencies contracting with the Social Security Administration to evaluate applications for disability and to determine eligibility for benefits.

Disability extension of coverage: Under many group health insurance plans, a right to remain covered without further payment of premiums for a designated time period (typically one year) if you are disabled at the time your group coverage comes to an end. The coverage remains in effect only for your medical expenses relating to your disability.

Disability waiver of premium: Provisions in insurance policies (typically life or disability coverage) allowing the coverage to remain in force without the payment of additional premiums after you have been disabled for a certain time.

Do not resuscitate (DNR) order: A document specifying your wishes that cardiopulmonary resuscitation not be administered to you in the event of coronary failure. Must be done in strict accordance with the requirements of your state. See also *living will.*

Elimination period: In disability policies, the time you must be disabled before benefits will start. Also referred to as *qualification period.*

Employee Retirement Income and Security Act of 1974 (ERISA): Federal legislation governing most legal disputes over employer-offered benefit plans, including health insurance. Historically, has caused problems because its broad terms and federal jurisdiction make many state laws, including those prohibiting discrimination, inapplicable. The 1996 health insurance reforms, however, amended the legislation to prohibit discrimination based on health status and other grounds.

Evidence of insurability: Generally, proof to the satisfaction of any insurance company with which you are applying for coverage that you are an acceptable insurance risk. Typically, being HIV-positive will disqualify you from further consideration.

Executor: The person in charge of administering an estate and following through with the *probate* process. Unless one provides otherwise in a will, blood relations are in most states given priority to serve. In some states, called a *personal representative*.

Family and Medical Leave Act of 1993: A federal law requiring employers of a certain size to allow their employees to take up to twelve weeks of unpaid leave per year if a serious health condition of the employee or the employee's child, spouse, or parent arises. During the time of absence, benefits must be preserved intact, and no demotion or other sanctions can result from the time off. The twelve weeks need not necessarily be taken consecutively.

Grace period: The extra time (often thirty days) provided under an insurance policy to make premium payments after their due date to keep coverage in force.

Guaranteed issue: Insurance coverage, generally health or life, made available without regard to the applicant's health status. Some states require that health insurers make such policies available on a limited basis. In the context of life insurance, such coverage often involves substantially higher premiums and disqualification for death benefits unless the insured lives for a defined amount of time after the issuance of the policy.

Guardian: An individual appointed by the court to act as a person's legal representative when that person has become physically or mentally incapacitated, or both. Can be named in advance through a designation of *preneed guardianship*.

Health care proxy: A person authorized by you in a legally recognized document to make medical decisions on your behalf if you become unable to make them for yourself. Depending on the state, may also be referred to as a *health care surrogate* or a durable power of attorney for health care.

Health care surrogate: See *health care proxy*.

High-risk pool: Programs certain states have established in order to make health insurance available to people who would otherwise be uninsurable. Such programs are typically administered by private insurance companies, but are heavily subsidized by the state. Coverage varies in quality, and premiums are often expensive.

HMO (health maintenance organization): An increasingly popular form of managed-care organization designed to cut health care costs, typically operating by requiring its members to use doctors within a certain network, compensating those doctors primarily through *capitation* formulas, limiting access to specialists, and sometimes restricting the use of certain medical treatments and procedures through the use of *preauthorization* clauses and otherwise. Compare with *PPO*.

Incontestability clause: Most common in life and disability insurance policies, such provisions limit an insurer's ability to challenge a policy for any reason except the nonpayment of premiums after it has been in place for a certain period of time, typically two years.

Individual underwriting: The process by which an insurance company evaluates an application for individual coverage, focusing on that person's specific health situation in order to assess its risk in extending the requested coverage.

ITF (in trust for): The designation of a beneficiary on a bank account or other financial account, by which ownership of the funds will automatically pass to the named person following the death of the account's owner. In some states, referred to as *payable on death (POD)* accounts.

Judgment proof: Lacking any property that creditors could successfully try to take from you, even if they had obtained the entry of a court judgment against you.

Living benefits: See *accelerated benefits*.

Living trust: See *trust*.

Living will: A document by which you can state your wish to be allowed to die and not kept alive by artificial means if you are in a terminal condition and are probably not coming out of it. May be supplemented with a *do not resuscitate (DNR) order.*

Medicaid: A federal-state medical assistance program offering health insurance coverage to the poor, disabled, and certain others. A means-based benefit, meaning that strict asset and income limitations apply. Covers prescriptions and hospitalizations, but its poor reimbursement rate to participating health care providers often results in problems with access to treatment and low quality care.

Medicare: Government health insurance covering people over sixty-five, the blind, and the long-term disabled. Consists of Part A coverage (hospital insurance) and Part B coverage (medical insurance). Monthly premiums must be paid only for Part B. Although coverage is generally superior to *Medicaid,* its major flaw is its lack of coverage for prescription drugs and certain other treatments.

Mini-COBRA laws: See *COBRA.*

Nonprobate assets: Assets which automatically pass to a chosen beneficiary after your death with no need for court involvement, such as life insurance proceeds and bank accounts, retirement plans, etc., for which you have designated a beneficiary.

Open enrollment: A period during which an insured can obtain new coverage, or increase or otherwise improve existing coverage, without *evidence of insurability.* In the context of employee benefits, such periods often last for a defined period after a new employee becomes eligible for coverage.

Patient's Self-Determination Act: A federal law requiring hospitals, nursing-home facilities, etc., to inform their patients upon admission of their rights under their state's law to designate a *health care proxy* and to sign a *living will.*

Payable on death (POD): See *ITF.*

Personal representative: See *executor*.

Portability: The ability to move from one job to another with no resulting gaps in health insurance coverage.

Power of attorney: A document, limited or broad in its scope, by which one person grants authority to another to take specific actions on his or her behalf. A durable power is one that is intended to remain in effect even if the person granting the power has become incapacitated. A springing power is one intended to take effect only upon the occurrence of a specified contingency. All such powers become immediately void upon the death of the person granting the power.

PPO (preferred provider organization): A type of managed-care organization sharing in common with *HMO*s its use of certain cost-cutting procedures, but allowing its participants greater access to specialists and more freedom to seek treatment outside of the network defined by the plan, albeit at a greater cost. Sometimes referred to as "point of service" plans.

Preauthorization: A technique typically used in managed care to help control health care costs, through which *HMO*s or *PPO*s agree to pay for nonemergency medical treatments or procedures only if prior approval has been requested and obtained from them for the treatments. Disputes often arise in this context when managed-care organizations decline to authorize a desired treatment on the basis that it is not "medically necessary."

Preexisting condition: In health or disability insurance, a medical condition for which benefits are delayed or excluded because it existed within a certain time prior to the effective date of the coverage.

Preneed guardianship: A document by which you can legally make known your wishes as to whom you would choose to have serve as your *guardian* if you ever became incapacitated.

Probate: The process of administering an estate in court after death, including filing the will (if any) with the court, having a *personal rep-*

resentative or *executor* appointed by a judge, notifying and paying creditors, if appropriate, and distributing the estate to beneficiaries. Process is required only to pass title to assets in sole name of person who has died, not *nonprobate assets.*

Qualification period: See *elimination period.*

Qualified viatical settlement provider: One of the prerequisites for the nontaxability of viatical settlement proceeds. If you live in a state requiring licensing, a viatical company must be licensed to fit into this category. If you do not, the company must abide by certain model legislation and regulations promulgated by the National Association of Insurance Commissioners. The federal law focuses on the qualifications of the company purchasing your policy, not on those of any broker involved.

Reasonable accommodations: If an employee with a disability requests that appropriate changes be made either to his or her job structure (such as changed hours, time off, etc.) or to the physical structure of the workplace in order to allow the employee to keep on working, the *ADA* requires that such changes be made if to do so will not impose an undue hardship upon the employer.

Reconsideration: The first level of social security appeals, requesting that the *DDS* revisit its initial conclusion that you are not disabled and therefore not eligible for benefits. If you are denied at this level, the next step is *administrative hearing.*

Rescission: The voiding of an insurance contract by the insurance company, in which coverage ceases and premiums previously paid are returned to you, on the basis it would never have issued the policy had full and accurate information been provided in your application.

Rights of survivorship: A form of ownership in which title to property automatically passes to the survivor upon the death of one owner. If two or more unmarried people own real property together and these words are not mentioned specifically on the deed, a *tenancy in common* results.

Social Security Disability Insurance (SSDI): A federal-sponsored disability insurance plan operated by the Social Security Administration paying you a certain amount per month during the period of your disability. To qualify, you must have sufficiently paid in to the system through social security payroll taxes (FICA), and the amount of your benefit will depend on your work history. In contrast to *SSI*, not a means-based asset and therefore no income or asset limitations apply. After two years, leads to *Medicare* coverage.

Supplemental Security Income (SSI): A federal welfare program operated by the Social Security Administration providing fixed monthly payments to disabled people with income and assets below a certain level. Automatically leads to *Medicaid* coverage, and possibly other means-based benefits as well.

Tenancy in common: A form of ownership involving no *rights of survivorship*. If property is held this way, ownership is automatically severed by the death of one party, and the share of the person who has died will pass to his or her estate rather than to the other owner.

Terminally ill individual: A prerequisite for the nontaxability of viatical settlement proceeds. To qualify, you must be certified by a physician as having a life expectancy of twenty-four months or less. You must also sell your policy to a qualified viatical settlement provider.

Trust: A legal document, often referred to as a *living trust*. By naming a trustee (often yourself) and a successor trustee (who takes over when you have become incapacitated or die), and transferring property into the trust, you are prepared for whatever happens. If you become incapacitated, your successor trustee will have access to the trust assets for your benefit, and following your death the trust will dictate who is to inherit your property. An extremely flexible tool in estate planning.

Undue influence: Grounds for attacking a *will* and other legal documents, arguing that the document does not reflect the true desires of the person signing it, but is rather the result of improper pressure applied by another person.

Viatication: The process of selling one's life insurance policy, or irrevocably assigning ownership of the policy to a viatical company or other investor in return for payment of an agreed percentage of its face value. After the seller (or "viator") dies, the purchaser receives the full proceeds of the policy, thus receiving the return on its investment. In contrast to *accelerated benefits,* viatical transactions involve deals with third-party viatical companies rather than the companies issuing the policies.

Will: A legal document, intended to take effect upon your death, specifying who will inherit your property, who will serve as the administrator (*personal representative,* or *executor*) of your estate, and related concerns.

APPENDIX B: RESOURCES FOR FURTHER INFORMATION AND ACCESS TO LEGAL REPRESENTATION

I. National Resources
II. Helpful Sites on the Internet
III. Topic-Specific Resources
IV. State HIV/AIDS Resources

Note: Although the following resources are intended to point you in the right direction, please be aware that we have done no investigation into any of them or otherwise evaluated the quality of their services. Thus, their inclusion here should not be construed as an endorsement. We hope they will help!

I. NATIONAL RESOURCES

CDC National AIDS Hotline	(800) 342-AIDS
CDC National AIDS Hotline/Spanish	(800) 344-SIDA
CDC National AIDS Information Clearinghouse	(800) 458-5231
National AIDS Hotline for Hearing Impaired	(800) 243-7889
National Clearinghouse for Alcohol and Drug Information	(800) 729-6686
National Native American AIDS Hotline	(800) 283-AIDS
National Teen AIDS Hotline	(800) 234-TEEN

American Bar Association AIDS Coordinating Committee
(Focus: providing advice and technical assistance to attorneys and judges confronting legal issues involving HIV)
Fifteenth Street, NW
ington, DC 20005-1009
2-1025

APPENDIX B: RESOURCES

American Civil Liberties Union
Lesbian and Gay Rights/AIDS Civil Liberties Project
132 West Forty-third Street
New York, NY 10036
(212) 944-9800

Gay and Lesbian Health Concerns
125 Worth Street
Box 67
New York, NY 10013
(212) 788-4308

Lambda Legal Defense and Education Fund
New York Office
666 Broadway
New York, NY 10012
(212) 995-8585

National Hemophilia Foundation
110 Greene Street
Suite 303
New York, NY
(212) 219-8180

Ryan White Foundation
1717 West Eighty-sixth Street
Suite 220
Indianapolis, IN 46260
(317) 876-1100 or (800) 444-7926

II. HELPFUL SITES ON THE INTERNET

Note: The following sites were accurate as of press time, but Internet sites change with great frequency. For updates, current information, and additional links, please visit the author's Web site at http://www.HIVLawToday.com

AIDS Law Updates http://www.thebody.com/hanssens/updates.html
(Lambda Legal Defense and Education Fund, with attorney Catherine Hanssens)

Employee Benefits Infosource http://www.ifebp.org/icebinfo.html
(General information on employee benefits, sponsored by the International Foundation of Employee Benefit Plans)

HIV InfoWeb Legal Information and Resources
http://www.jri.org/infoweb/legal/
(General information on HIV/AIDS and the law)

Prison Law Links http://www.wco.com/%7Eaerick/links.htm
(Contains several links relating to HIV and prison issues)

The Viatical Settlement Page http://www.global.org/viatical/
(General information/updates on the viatical industry, sponsored by the Viatical Association of America)

Welcome to Social Security Online http://www.ssa.gov/
(Great information on the Social Security Administration)

III. TOPIC-SPECIFIC RESOURCES

Employment Health Insurance Issues

National Business Coalition on Health
1015 Eighteenth Street, NW
Suite 450
Washington, DC 20036
(202) 775-9300

Guardianship/Children's Issues

Child Welfare League of America
Task Force on Children and HIV Infection
440 First Street, NW
Suite 310
Washington, DC 20001-2085
(202) 638-2952

Sunburst National AIDS Project
P.O. Box 2824
Petaluma, CA 94952
(707) 769-0169

APPENDIX B: RESOURCES   215

HIV and the Elderly

Senior Action in a Gay Environment (SAGE)
305 Seventh Avenue
New York, NY 10012
(212) 741-2247

Immigration

American Immigration Lawyers Association
1400 Eye Street, NW
Suite 1200
Washington, DC 20005
(202) 371-9377

National Migrant Resource Program, Inc.
1515 South Capitol of Texas Highway
Suite 220
Austin, TX 78746
(512) 328-7682

Medicare and Related Health Insurance Issues

Medicare Rights Center Hotline
6 Prospect Street
Midland Park, NJ 07432
(212) 869-3850 or (800) 333-4114

Right to Die Issues, Access to Living Will Forms

Choice in Dying, Inc.
P.O. Box 397
Newark, NJ 07101
(800) 989-WILL

Social Security Disability Issues

National Organization of Social Security Claimants' Representatives
(800) 431-2804

Veterans' Issues

Department of Veterans Administration Information Line
(800) 827-1000

Women's Issues

National Black Women's Health Project
1211 Connecticut Avenue
Washington, DC 20036
(202) 835-0117

National Women's Health Network
514 Tenth Street, NW
#400
Washington, DC 20036
(202) 835-0117

Radical Women
32 Union Square East
Suite 907
New York, NY 10003
(212) 677-7002

IV. STATE HIV/AIDS RESOURCES

Alabama

Alabama AIDS Hotline
434 Monroe Street
Montgomery, AL 36130-3017
(800) 228-0469 or (334) 613-5357

Alaska

Alaskan AIDS Assistance Association HIV/AIDS Hotline
1057 West Fireweed Lane
#102
Anchorage, AK 99503
(800) 478-2437 or (907) 263-2052

Arizona

Arizona AIDS Hotline
4460 North Central Avenue
Phoenix, AZ 85012
(602) 265-3300

APPENDIX B: RESOURCES

HIV/AIDS Law Project (HALP)
Maricopa County Bar Association
303 East Palm Lane
Phoenix, AZ 85004
(602) 258-3434

Arkansas

Arkansas AIDS Hotline
4815 Markham Street
Slot 33
Little Rock, AR 72205-3867
(501) 661-2408

California (Northern)

Berkeley Community Law Center
3130 Shattuck Avenue
Berkeley, CA 94705-1823
(510) 548-4040

AIDS Legal Referral Panel of the San Francisco Bay Area
114 Sansome Street
Suite 1129
San Francisco, CA 94104
(415) 291-5454

Immigrant HIV Assistance Project
685 Market Street
Suite 700
San Francisco, CA 94103
(415) 267-0795

Legal Services for Children
1254 Market Street
San Francisco, CA 94103
(415) 764-1600

Northern California HIV/AIDS Hotline
10 United Nations Plaza
Suite 405
San Francisco, CA 94102
(415) 487-8000 or (800) 367-2437

Project Inform
1965 Market Street
Suite 220
San Francisco, CA 94103
(800) 822-7422

California (Southern)

AIDS Project—Los Angeles
1313 North Vine Street
Los Angeles, CA 90028
(213) 993-1600

Barristers Hospice/AIDS Project
P.O. Box 55020
Los Angeles, CA
(213) 896-6436

Elizabeth Taylor Foundation
P.O. Box 17160
Los Angeles, CA 90017
(301) 472-7778

Lambda Legal Defense & Education Fund
6030 Wilshire Boulevard
Suite 200
Los Angeles, CA 90036-3617
(213) 937-2728

Southern California HIV/AIDS Hotline
1313 North Vine Street
Los Angeles, CA 90028-8107
(800) 922-2437

AIDS Foundation San Diego
140 Arbor Drive
San Diego, CA 92103
(619) 686-5050

Colorado

Colorado AIDS Hotline
4300 Cherry Creek Drive, South
Suite A-3
Denver, CO 80222-1530
(303) 782-9186 or (800) 252-2437

APPENDIX B: RESOURCES

Colorado AIDS Project
P.O. Box 18529
Denver, CO 80218
(303) 837-0166

Connecticut

Connecticut Department of Health
 and Human Services
150 Washington Street
Hartford, CT 06106
(860) 509-7806 or (800) 203-1234

Delaware

Delaware AIDS Hotline
601 Delaware Avenue
#5
Wilmington, DE 19801-1452
(302) 652-6776 or (800) 422-0429

District of Columbia

DC AIDS Information Line
1407 S Street, NW
Washington, DC 20009-3819
(202) 939-7822

Deaf AIDS Action
813 L Street, SE
Washington, DC 20003
(202) 546-9768 (TTY/TDD)

District of Columbia School of Law HIV Legal Clinic
4250 Connecticut Avenue, NW
Washington, DC 20008
(202) 274-7330

Whitman-Walker Clinic Legal Services Project
1407 S Street, NW
Washington, DC 20009
(202) 797-3527; (202) 328-0697 (Spanish); (202) 797-3575
(TTY/TDD)

Florida

AIDS Help, Inc.
P.O. Box 4374
Key West, FL 33304
(305) 296-6196

Haitian American Community Association of Dade County
Minority AIDS Program
8037 NE Second Avenue
Miami, FL 33138
(305) 751-3429

Health Crisis Network
5050 Biscayne Boulevard
Miami, FL 33137
(305) 751-7751 (Hotline)

Legal Services of Greater Miami AIDS Advocacy Project
3000 Biscayne Boulevard
Suite 500
Miami, FL 33137
(305) 576-0080

Volunteer Lawyers Program/Dade County Bar Association
123 NW First Avenue
Miami, FL 33128
(305) 579-5733

Big Bend Comprehensive AIDS Resources
P.O. Box 14365
Tallahassee, FL 33231
(904) 656-2437

Florida HIV/AIDS Hotline
P.O. Box 20169
Tallahassee, FL 32316-0169
(904) 681-9131 or (800) FLA-AIDS

Georgia

AIDS Legal Project
Atlanta Legal AID Society
151 Springs Street NW
Atlanta, GA 30303
(404) 614-3969

Georgia AIDS Information Line
1438 West Peachtree Street
Atlanta, GA 30309-2955
(404) 885-6800 or (800) 551-2728

Hawaii

Hawaii STD/AIDS Hotline
277 Ohua Avenue
Honolulu, HI 96815-3643
(800) 321-1555

Idaho

Idaho AIDS Foundation Hotline
1035 Lusk Street
Boise, ID 83706-2832
(800) 677-2437

Illinois

AIDS Legal Council of Chicago
220 South State Street
Suite 2030
Chicago, IL 60604
(312) 427-8990

Illinois AIDS Hotline
961 West Montana Street
Chicago, IL 60614-2408
(312) 472-6469 or (800) AID-AIDS

Lambda Legal Defense & Education Fund
17 East Monroe
Suite 212
Chicago, IL 60603
(312) 759-8110

Indiana

Indiana Cares
3951 North Meridian Street
Suite 101
Indianapolis, IN 46208
(317) 920-1200

Indiana Community AIDS Action Network (ICAN)
3951 North Meridian Street
Suite 200
Indianapolis, IN 46208
(317) 920-3190 or (800) 659-7580

Indiana STD/AIDS Hotline
2 North Meridian Street
Indianapolis, IN 46204
(317) 233-7840 or (317) 233-1325

Iowa

Iowa Statewide AIDS Hotline
2116 Grand Avenue
Des Moines, IA 50312-5368
(515) 244-6700 or (800) 445-2437

Kentucky

Kentucky AIDS Hotline
214 West Maxwell Street
Lexington, KY 40585
(800) 840-2865

Louisiana

Capital Area Legal Services
200 Third Street
Baton Rouge, LA 70802
(800) 256-1900

Acadiana Legal Services Corp.
P.O. Box 4823
Lafayette, LA 70501
(318) 237-4320 or (800) 256-1175

AIDSLaw of Louisiana, Inc.
P.O. Box 30203
New Orleans, LA 70190
(504) 944-5035

Louisiana AIDS Hotline
1407 Decatur Street
New Orleans, LA 70116
(504) 944-2437 or (800) 99AIDS9

APPENDIX B: RESOURCES 223

Maine

Maine AIDS Coalition
615 West Congress Street
Portland, ME 04101-4031
(800) 851-2437 or (800) 775-1267

Maryland

Maryland AIDS Hotline
11141 Georgia Avenue
Suite 312
Wheaton, MD 20902-4658
(410) 333-2437 or (800) 638-6252 (MD only); (800) 322-7432 (VA/DC only)

Massachusetts

Gay and Lesbian Advocates and Defenders AIDS Law Project
P.O. Box 218
Boston, MA 02112
(617) 426-1350

Massachusetts AIDS Action Hotline
131 Clarendon Street
Fifteenth Floor
Boston, MA 02116-5131
(617) 437-6200 or (800) 235-2331

Legal Services Center, AIDS Law Clinic
122 Boyleston Street
Jamaica Plain, MA 02130
(617) 522-3003

Michigan

AIDS Legal Referral Service
916 Ford Building
Detroit, MI 48226
(313) 964-4188

Michigan AIDS Hotline
845 Livernois
Ferndale, MI 48220-2308
(810) 547-3783 or (800) 872-2437

Michigan Protection & Advocacy Center
   HIV/AIDS Advocacy Program
(800) 288-5923 or (800) 414-3956

Minnesota

Minnesota AIDS Project Legal Program
1400 Park Avenue, South
Minneapolis, MN 55404-1550
(612) 373-2426 or (800) 248-2437

Mississippi

Mississippi AIDS Hotline
P.O. Box 5192
Jackson, MS 39296-5192
(601) 936-8990 or (800) 826-2961

Missouri

Missouri Department of Health AIDS Information Line
1730 Elm Street
Jefferson City, MO 65102
(573) 751-6141 or (800) 533-2437

Legal Aid of Western Missouri AIDS Legal Assistance Program
1005 Grand
Suite 600
Kansas City, MO 64106
(816) 474-6750

Legal Services of Eastern Missouri, Inc./AIDS Project
4232 Forest Park Avenue
St. Louis, MO 63108
(314) 367-1700

Montana

Montana AIDS Program
Cogswell Building
Helena, MT 59620
(406) 444-3566

APPENDIX B: RESOURCES

Nebraska

Nebraska AIDS Hotline
3610 Dodge Street
Suite 110-W
Omaha, NE 68105
(402) 342-6367 or (402) 342-4233

Nevada

Nevada AIDS Hotline
505 East King Street
Room 304
Carson City, NV 89710
(800) 842-2437

New Hampshire

New Hampshire AIDS Hotline
Health & Welfare Building
6 Hazen Drive
Concord, NH 03301-6501
(603) 271-4502 or (800) 752-2437

New Jersey

Hyacinth AIDS Foundation
Jersey City, NJ
(800) 433-0254 or (201) 432-1134

New Jersey AIDS Hotline
201 Lyons Avenue
Newark, NJ 07112-2027
(800) 624-2377

New Mexico

New Mexico AIDS Hotline
1190 St. Francis Drive
Santa Fe, NM 87505-6110
(800) 545-2437

New York

New York State HIV/AIDS Hotlines
RPCI, RSC-4
Elm & Carlton Streets

Buffalo, NY 14263-0001
(716) 845-3170 or (800) 541-2437

Gay Men's Health Crisis Department of Legal Services
129 West Twentieth Street
New York, NY 10011-3629
(212) 337-3504 or (212) 807-6655

HIV Law Project
841 Broadway
Suite 608
New York, NY 10003
(212) 674-7590

Legal AID Society/Volunteers Division/Community Law Offices
230 East 106th Street
New York, NY 10029
(212) 722-2000

New York Division of Human Rights
  Office/AIDS Discrimination Issues
55 West 125th Street
Twelfth Floor
New York, NY 10027
(800) 523-2437 (Hotline)

New York Lawyers for the Public Interest
135 East 15th Street
New York, NY 10003
(212) 727-2270

Prisoner's Legal Services of New York
105 Chambers Street
Second Floor
New York, NY 10007
(212) 513-7373

Volunteers of Legal Service AIDS Project
17 Varick Street
Fifteenth Floor
New York, NY 10013
(212) 966-4400

New York State HIV Counseling Hotline
(800) 872-2777

APPENDIX B: RESOURCES

North Dakota

North Dakota AIDS Hotline
600 East Boulevard Avenue
Bismarck, ND 58505-0200
(800) 472-2180

Ohio

AIDS Task Force of Greater Cleveland
2250 Euclid Avenue
Cleveland, OH 44115
(216) 621-0766

Ohio AIDS Hotline
1500 West Third Avenue
Suite 329
Columbus, OH 43212-2856
(614) 488-2437 or (800) 332-2437

Oklahoma

Oklahoma AIDS Hotline
1000 NE Tenth Street
Mail Drop 0308
Oklahoma City, OK 73117-1299
(415) 271-4636 or (800) 535-AIDS

Oregon

Oregon AIDS Hotline
(Cascade AIDS Foundation)
620 SW Fifth Avenue
Suite 300
Portland, OR 97204-1418
(503) 223-5907 or (800) 777-2437

Pennsylvania

Pennsylvania Department of Health Bureau of HIV/AIDS
Forrester & Commonwealth Avenues
H&W Building
Room 912
Harrisburg, PA 17120
(717) 783-0479 or (800) 662-6080

AIDS Law Project of Pennsylvania
1211 Chestnut Street
Suite 1200
Philadelphia, PA
(215) 587-9377

Rhode Island

Rhode Island Project AIDS Hotline
95 Chestnut Street
Third Floor
Providence, RI 02903-4161
(401) 831-5522 or (800) 726-3010

South Carolina

South Carolina Department of Health AIDS Hotline
Robert Mills Complex
Box 101106
Columbia, SC 29211
(803) 737-4110 or (800) 322-2437

South Dakota

South Dakota AIDS Hotline
445 East Capitol Avenue
Pierre, SD 57501-3185
(800) 592-1861

Tennessee

Tennessee AIDS Hotline
Tennessee Tower
Thirteenth Floor
SE 312 Eighth North
Nashville, TN 37247-4947
(615) 741-7500 or (800) 525-2437

Texas

Texas AIDSLINE
Texas Department of Public Health Promotion
1100 West Forty-ninth Street
Austin, TX 78756-3101
(512) 458-7111 or (800) 299-2437

APPENDIX B: RESOURCES

AIDS Legal Network Community Outreach Center
1125 West Peter Smith
Fort Worth, TX 76104
(817) 335-3617

Houston Bar Association AIDS Committee
Williams, Bernberg & Andersen
6671 Southwest Freeway
Suite 303
Houston, TX 77074-2209
(713) 981-9595

AIDS Legal Assistance—Texas
(800) 828-6417

Utah

Utah AIDS Information Hotline
1408 South 1100 East
Salt Lake City, UT 84105-2435
(801) 487-2323 or (800) 366-2437

Vermont

Vermont Department of Health
108 Cherry Street
Burlington, VT 05402
(802) 863-7245 or (800) 882-AIDS

Virgin Islands

Virgin Islands AIDS Hotline
6&7 Estate Diamond & Ruby
Christiansted, VI 00820
(809) 778-6105 or (809) 773-2437

Virginia

Virginia AIDS Hotline
P.O. Box 2448
Room 112
Richmond, VA 23218-2448
(804) 487-2323 or (800) 533-4148

Washington

Washington HIV/AIDS Hotline
Airdustrial Park, Building 9
MS 47840
Olympia, WA 98504-7840
(360) 586-3887 or (800) 272-AIDS

Volunteer Attorneys for Persons with AIDS Legal Referral Project
600 Bank of California Building
900 Fourth Avenue
Seattle, WA 98164
(206) 624-9365

West Virginia

West Virginia AIDS Program
1422 Washington Street, East
Charleston, WV 25301-1978
(304) 558-2950 or (800) 642-8244

Wisconsin

AIDS Resource Center of Wisconsin, Inc.
Legal Assistance Program
P.O. Box 92487
Milwaukee, WI 53202
(414) 224-1554
Wisconsin AIDS Hotline
P.O. Box 92505
Milwaukee, WI 53202-0505
(414) 273-1991 or (800) 334-2437

Wyoming

Wyoming AIDS Hotline
Hathaway Building
Fourth Floor
2300 Capitol Avenue
Cheyenne, WY 82002-0710
(307) 777-5800 or (800) 327-3577

INDEX

Accelerated benefits, 167–68, 202, 211
Administrative hearing, 145, 147–50, 202, 209
Administrative law judge (ALJ), 145, 147–50, 202, 209
Aid to Families with Dependent Children (AFDC), 138
AIDS hotline, 116, 212 (*see also* Resources, directory of)
Americans with Disabilities Act of 1990 (ADA), 119, 192, 193, 199
  provisions, 187–90, 202, 209
Appeals:
  disability designation, 144, 147–50, 202, 209
  managed-care rights, 127
Automatic stay, 161

Bankruptcy, 160–63
  alternatives to, 151–59
  Chapter 7, 160–62, 202
  debts exempt from, 162–63
  defined, 202
  drawbacks of, 151–52
  options, 160
  timing of, 163
  trustee, 162–63
Banks, 50–54
  automatic payment services, 54, 72
  creditor attachment of account, 154
  direct deposit, 53–54
  durable power of attorney honored by, 49
  ITF/POD accounts, 52–53, 206
  joint account's pros and cons, 51–52, 54
Beneficiary:
  of life insurance policy, 78–79, 170
  naming of, 32
  nonprobate assets and, 207
Benefits payments:
  coordination of, 83–84, 203
  direct deposit of, 53–54
  disability amounts and duration, 83
  lifetime caps, 100, 118
  SSD waiting period, 129, 131, 136, 141
  SSI non-waiting period, 131
  taxability of, 85
Bills, automatic payment of, 54
Birth certificate, 142
Blood test irregularities code, 87, 88
Broker company (viatical settlement), 170–73

Capitation (managed-care), 124–25, 203, 206
Cardiopulmonary resuscitation, 61–62, 204
Car ownership, 155, 162
CDC hotline, 116, 212
Certified letter, 109, 158
Chapter 7 bankruptcy, 160–63, 202
Choice in Dying, Inc., 61
Chronically ill individual, tax definition of, 178–79
COBRA (Consolidated Omnibus Budget Reconciliation Act of 1985), 13, 102, 109–13

COBRA (*cont.*)
  applicability only to health insurance, 78
  conversion to individual policy under, 110
  creditable coverage and, 97–98
  defined, 203
  disability dating and, 107–9, 140–41
  disability extension and, 113
  eligibility, 106–7
  specific benefits kept in force by, 105
Codes:
  Medical Information Bureau, 87–88
  proper use on HMO claim forms, 126
Confidentiality:
  insurance claims, 85–89
  workplace, 192–93, 194–95
Consumer-credit counseling service, 152–53
Contract, preneed, 19–20
Conversion insurance coverage, 110–12, 203
  conversion period, 112
  disability extension and, 113
Coordination of benefits, 83–84, 203
Creditable coverage, 97, 101–8, 203
Credit cards, 163
Creditors, 151–59
  automatic stay, 161
  bankruptcy declaration, 160–63, 202
  judgment-proof status, 153, 155, 156–59, 206
  prioritizing, 153, 163
  property exemptions, 155, 162
  secured, 154, 156, 162
Credit rating, 151, 156
Death:
  do not resuscitate order, 61–62, 204
  durable power of attorney ended by, 47
  living will and, 59–62
  terminal condition definition, 60
  See also Estate planning; Life expectancy
Death benefits, 32–33
  life insurance, 78–79
  social security, 130
Diary, 134, 135
Direct deposit, 53–54
Direct transfer payments, 54, 72
Disability dating, 108–9, 140–41
Disability Determination Services (DDS), 143, 146, 148, 202, 203, 209
Disability insurance, 79–85
  benefits, amount and duration, 83
  benefits, coordination of, 83–84, 203
  COBRA and, 105, 107–9, 140, 203
  definitions in policy, 82–85
  documentation for, 80, 134
  extension of coverage, 111, 112–13, 204
  Health Claims Index, 89
  incontestability clause, 73–74, 206
  Medicare coverage and, 110
  payments' exemption from creditors, 156
  periodic medical exams and, 84–85
  preexisting condition and, 208
  recurrent disability and, 84
  SSA dating of disability and, 108–9, 140–41
  SSDI as supplement to, 128
  taxation of benefits, 85
  timing of benefits filing, 81
  waiting period, 83, 204
  waiver of premium, 76, 83, 204
  See also Social Security Disability Insurance
Discrimination, 119, 185–93
  ERISA and, 204
  specific legal rights, 189–92, 194–97, 200, 202
  suit filing, 193, 196
  suit's effects on SSDI benefits, 139–40

Divorce, 116
Documentation
  of disability, 80, 134
    importance in SSDI appeals process, 147, 148
    medical record as, 80, 134, 148
    Social Security benefits application requirements, 142
Document safeguards, 63–68
Do not resuscitate (DNR) order, 61–62, 204 (*see also* Living will)
Drugs:
  diary record of prescribed, 135
  disability insurance and, 84–85
  health insurance coverage for, 93, 96
  managed-care limits for, 122–23
  Medicaid coverage for, 133
  Medicare noncoverage for, 110–11, 112, 132, 207
  off-label uses, 78
  treatment breakthroughs and viatical settlements, 166, 175, 176, 177
  workplace testing for, 191
Durable power of attorney, 46–49, 205, 208

Elimination period:
  disability benefits, 83, 129, 131, 141, 204
  insurance coverage, 76, 84
Employment, 194–200
  Americans with Disabilities Act rights, 187–90, 202
  COBRA provisions, 104–11, 203
  ERISA provisions, 117–19
  Family and Medical Leave Act rights, 197–99, 205
  and health insurance portability, 96, 101–2, 208
  preemployment, pre-offer stage, 189, 190–91
  preemployment, postoffer stage, 189, 192
  postemployment, 189,192
  "reasonable accommodations" provision, 188–89, 193, 197, 202, 209
  self-protective measures, 195–97
  workplace drug testing, 191
  See also Disability insurance; Discrimination; Group insurance
Equal Employment Opportunity Commission (EEOC), 119, 193
ERISA (Employee Retirement Income and Security Act of 1974), 117–19, 204
Estate planning:
  bank account management, 50–54, 206
  executor naming, 18, 204–5
  importance of wills, 15–23
  nonprobate assets, 207
  probate and, 30–31, 208–9
  property assessment and, 29–33
  reasons for, 15–18
  trusts and, 24–28, 210
  See also Will
Executor, 18, 204–5, 209, 211
Experimental treatments, 77–78

Family and Medical Leave Act of 1993 (FMLA), 197–99, 205
Food and Drug Administration, 77–78
Food stamps, 131, 138, 143
Form 4814 (SSA), 129–30, 136
Funeral wishes, 18–20

"Gatekeeper" (primary-care physician), 123–25, 126
Grace period, 77, 205
Group insurance:
  availability and access, 99–100
  claim filing and privacy concerns, 195
  COBRA rights, 104–11, 203
  conversion to individual policy, 111–12, 203
  creditable coverage and, 101–2, 203

Group insurance (*cont.*)
  disability extension of coverage, 113, 204
  ERISA and, 117–19
  Family and Medical Leave Act rights and, 197–99
  "guaranteed availability" of, 95
  legal protections under, 94–98
  less scrutiny of individual health records by, 90, 94
  outside company vs. self-funded, 117–18
  portability, 96, 101–2, 208
  practical workings of, 117–19
  renewability, 100–3
  risk spreading, 94, 101
  seeking coverage under, 114
  for small businesses and groups, 115
  special enrollment periods, 98
  viatication of own policy and, 170
Guardian, 38–44
  advance choice of, 41–42, 43
  coguardianship, 41
  defined, 205
  for incapacitated person, 38–41
  for minor children, 20, 42–44
  preneed, 43, 205, 208

Handicap, HIV infection classification as, 119, 186–87
Health care:
  experimental treatments coverage, 77–78
  living will and, 59–62
  managed-care provisions, 120–27, 206
  Medical Information Bureau and, 86–91
  periodic exams for disability insurance, 84–85
  preauthorization clauses, 122, 206, 208
  right to reject all treatment, 58
Health care proxy, 55–58, 205, 207
Health Claims Index, 89

Health insurance, 92–127
  basic coverage options, 93–94
  basic questions, 92–93
  claims confidentiality, 85–89
  COBRA rights, 104–11, 203
  conversion from group to individual policy, 111–12, 203
  coordination of benefits, 83–84, 203
  creditable coverage concept, 97, 101–2, 203
  employer's handling of, 117–19
  ERISA rights, 117–19, 204
  Family and Medical Leave Act rights, 197–99
  group availability and access, 99–100
  group membership protections, 90, 94–95
  group renewability, 100–3
  guaranteed issue, 205
  high-risk pool, 115, 205–6
  individual access, 101–3
  lifetime benefits caps, 100
  1996 reform legislation, 13, 94–104, 168
  open enrollment periods, 96, 114, 207
  options for uninsured HIV-positives, 114–17
  portability provisions, 96, 101–2, 208
  preexisting condition, 95–97, 208
  premium payments, 105–6
  spousal coverage, 116–17
  veterans' benefits, 116
  viatication and, 170
  See also Disability insurance; Group insurance; Managed-care organizations
Health Insurance Portability and Accountability Act of 1996, 13, 94–104, 168
  COBRA rights changes' under, 108
  improvement for individual health insurance applicant, 101–2

INDEX

preexisting condition definition, 96
and tax status of viatical settlements, 177
High-risk pool (health insurance), 115, 205–6
HIV-related illness:
"chronically ill" diagnosis for, 178
confidentiality status, 192–93, 194–95
diagnosis of, 88
discrimination and, 185–86, 200
employment survival guide, 194–200
factors in disability determination, 133–34, 148
financial drain of, 151, 165
legal status as "handicap," 119, 186–87
managed-care challenge in treating, 122–27
Medicare services, 132
opportunistic infections, 136
remission, 84, 144
Social Security Disability Insurance benefits and, 128–50
state resources, listing of, 216–30
See also Viatication; *other specific aspects*

Incapacity:
bank account management and, 50–54
health care proxy for, 55–58, 205
insurance premium payment continuation and, 72, 105
living will and, 59–60
planning ahead for, 38–42, 205
powers of attorney and, 45–49, 208
preneed guardianship and, 43, 205, 208
relatives' charges of, 65–67
successor trustee for, 24, 25–28, 41, 210
See also Disability insurance
Incontestability clause, 73–74, 206

Indigency, definition of, 116
Individual health insurance, 101–3
Individual underwriting, 206
Insurance, 69–91
claims confidentiality, 85–89
"coordination of benefits" provision, 83–84
dealing with companies, 69–70
definitions, 73–78
disability waiver of premiums, 76, 83, 204
effective dates for group and individual legal reforms, 95
ERISA provisions and, 117–19
evidence of insurability, 77, 204
familiarity with coverage, 70–72, 122, 126
guaranteed issue, 205
incontestability clause, 73–74, 206
individual underwriting, 206
keeping up premium payments, 72, 77, 97
Medical Information Bureau and, 86–91
open enrollment period, 78, 114, 207
"overinsurance" seekers, 89
recission, 74–75, 209
understanding "definitions" section, 71, 82–85
See also Benefits payments; Disability insurance; Group insurance; Health insurance; Life insurance; Premium payments; Social Security Disability Insurance
Internet:
author's Web site number, 14
helpful sites, 213–14
In trust for (ITF) bank accounts, 52–53, 206

"Job lock," preexisting condition and, 95–98
Joint bank accounts, 51–52, 54
Joint guardians, 41

Joint ownership, 31–32
    survivorship rights, 209
    unmarried home title, 34–35
    See also Tenancy in common
Joint tenantship with survivorship rights, 34
Judgment-proof status, 153, 155, 156–59, 206

Lawyer:
    for dealing with creditors, 153–54, 155
    for employment discrimination case, 192–93
    fees for filing personal bankruptcy, 161
    free services, 14, 22–23
    as guardian, 39–40
    for personal bankruptcy declaration, 160, 161, 162, 163
    providing safeguards in granting powers of attorney, 48
    for sale of own insurance policy, 165
    for SSDI appeals process, 145–46, 149
    unnecessary for health care proxy designation, 57
    for will preparation, 22–23
Leave, unpaid, 198–99, 205
Licensed viatical settlement providers, 179–80, 209
Life expectancy, viatical settlements and, 166–67, 168, 174–75, 176, 182, 211
Life insurance, 78–79
    accelerated benefits option, 167–68
    beneficiary, 78–79
    COBRA nonapplicability to, 105
    conversion, 78
    disability waiver of premiums, 204
    guaranteed issue, 205
    incontestability clause, 73–74, 206
    increasing, 78
    keeping up premium payments, 72–73, 166
    proceeds' exemption from creditors, 155–56, 162
    selling own, 76–77, 164–84, 209, 210, 211
    as superb asset, 166
    waiver of premium, 76, 83, 105
Life partner:
    dealing with incapacity of, 40–41
    as health care proxy, 57
    joint bank account with, 51–52
    lack of legal rights, 16–17
    safeguarding disposition documents for, 67
    "undue influence" claims against, 64–65
Lifetime benefits caps, 100, 118
Living benefits. *See* Accelerated benefits
Living trust, 23–24, 210
Living will, 56, 59–62, 207
    copies of, 58
    do not resuscitate order and, 61–62, 204
    naming agent, 57, 61

Managed-care organizations, 120–27
    appeals rights, 127
    basics of, 121–23
    capitation system, 124–25, 203, 206
    familiarity with provisions of, 122, 126–27
    HIV-positive patients' challenges to, 122–27
    HMOs as, 206
    Medicare and, 111, 132
    outside-the-network doctors and, 122
    PPOs and, 208
    practical tips in dealing with, 125–27
    preauthorization clauses, 122, 206, 208
    primary physician, 123–24, 126

Material misrepresentation, definition of, 74
Medicaid, 92, 97, 102, 143
  creditable coverage and, 203
  defined, 207
  loss after viatication, 170
  "presumptively disabled" finding and, 130
  Supplemental Security Income and, 138, 210
  workings of, 133
Medical Information Bureau (MIB), 86–91
Medical record:
  as disability claims verification, 80, 134–35, 148
  health insurers' review of, 89, 93
  Medical Information Bureau codes for, 87–88
  for Supplemental Security Income application, 142
"Medical Report on Adult with Allegation of HIV Infection" (SSA Form 4814), 129–30, 136
Medicare, 97, 102, 107–8, 207
  creditable coverage and, 203
  HMOs under, 111, 132
  qualification and end of COBRA coverage, 110, 112
  SSDI benefits leading to automatic qualification for, 130, 210
  workings of, 132–33, 207
Medicare Rights Center Hotline, 116, 132
Mental capacity:
  claims of lack of, 65–67
  creating record of, 66
  guardianship and, 38–41, 205
  See also Incapacity
Mini-COBRA laws, 106, 203
Mortgage payments, 162

National Association of Insurance Commissioners, 180, 182, 209
National legal-aid resources, directory of, 212–13

National Organization of Social Security Claimants' Representatives, 146
Nursing home coverage, 133

Office of Hearings and Appeals (OHA), 147–48
Open enrollment period:
  defined, 207
  health insurance, 96
  life insurance, 78
  state laws' requiring, 114

Patient's Self-Determination Act, 56, 207
Payable on death (POD) accounts, 52–53, 207
Personal finances:
  bankruptcy basics, 160–63, 202
  cash raised by selling own life insurance policy, 164–84
  dealing with creditors, 151–59
  delegating powers of attorney, 45–49
  See also Banks; Estate planning; Will
Phone numbers:
  government health care services, 115, 116
  Medicare Rights, 132
  national resources, 212–13
  Social Security Administration, 133, 141
  state HIV/AIDS resources, 216–30
  topic-specific, 214–16
  Viatical Association of America, 172
POD (payable on death) accounts, 52–53, 207
Portability provisions, 96, 101–2, 208
"Pour over" will, 24
Powers of attorney, 45–49
  advantages vs. disadvantages, 47
  defined, 208
  durable powers, 46–49, 205, 208
  funeral wishes and, 20

Powers of attorney (*cont.*)
    health care proxy and, 55–58, 205
    and keeping up insurance premium payments, 72
    limited vs. unlimited authority, 45–46, 208
    protection from abuses of, 48
    reversibility of, 49
Preauthorization clauses (medical treatment), 122, 206, 208
Preexisting conditions
    creditable coverage, 97, 101–2, 203
    definition of, 96, 208
    exclusions, 75–76
    legal protections for, 13, 95–98, 203
Prehearing memorandum, 148–49
Premium payments:
    COBRA continuation coverage and, 105–6, 107, 109–10
    creditable coverage and, 102
    disability waiver of, 76, 83, 204
    grace period, 77, 205
    high-risk pools, 115
    keeping up with, 72, 77, 102
    legal protection against individual rate variations, 99
    for Medicare Part B coverage, 132
    return under recission, 74–75, 209
    for SSDI program, 129
Premium waiver, 76, 83, 204
Preneed contract, 19–20
Preneed guardianship, 42–43, 205, 208
Presumptively disabled, 129–30, 136
Primary-care doctor, 123–25, 126
Privacy rights, 191, 192–93, 194–95
Probate:
    avoidance of, 30–31
    definition of, 30, 208–9
    executor and, 204–5, 209
    joint bank accounts and, 51
    nonprobate assets, 207
Probationary period (insurance), 76
Pro bono legal services, 14, 22–23

Property:
    assessment of, 29–33
    assets and SSI eligibility determination, 130
    creditor attachment and levy of, 154
    exemptions from creditors, 153–54, 155–56, 162, 206
    home ownership title, 34–37
    naming guardian of, 41
    survivorship rights, 209
Protease inhibitors, 95, 166, 177
Proxy, health care, 55–58, 205, 207
    living will agent vs., 61
    see also Powers of attorney
Public accommodations, 202

Qualified viatical settlement provider, 179–80, 209, 211

Real property, 29–30
    creditor's lien against, 154
    rights of survivorship, 209
Reasonable accommodations provision, 188–89, 193, 197, 202, 209
Recission, 74–75, 209
Reconsideration, 209
Recurrent disability, 84
Remission
    disability payments and, 84
    SSA trial work period and, 143–44
Representative payee, 54
Resources, directory of, 212–30
    Internet sites, 213–14
    national, 212–13
    topic-specific, 214–16
Revocation, of powers of attorney, 49
Risk spreading, 94, 101
Ryan White Act, 72, 115–16

Salary, benefits vs., 114
Second opinion, 149, 199
Secured creditors, 154, 156, 162
Siblings, legal property rights of, 16
Single parent, child's guardianship provision by, 42, 43

INDEX

Social Security Administration (SSA)
  glossary and timetable, 128–33
  Medicare coverage and, 132–33
  Office of Hearings and Appeals, 147–48
  phone number, 133, 141
  See also Disability Determination Services; Social Security Disability Insurance
Social security card, 142
Social Security Disability Insurance (SSDI), 128–50
  administrative hearing, 145, 146, 147–50, 202, 209
  appeals process, 144–50, 202, 209
  application procedure, 141–43
  defined, 210
  direct deposit of payments, 53–54
  eligibility for, 133, 203
  elimination period, 129, 131, 141, 204
  estimate of projected future benefits, 137
  Form 4814 and, 129–30, 136
  HIV-positive eligibility status, 133–37
  loss from failure to apply for, 130
  and Medicare eligibility, 107–8, 110, 130
  payments as creditor-exempt, 156
  "presumptively disabled" finding, 130, 136
  and private supplemental insurance, 79
  qualification credits, 129
  question number 3A, 140
  reconsideration, 209
  representative payee, 54
  retroactivity of, 141
  starting date, 140–41
  strategy in dealing with, 133–37
  Supplemental Security Income vs., 129, 130–32, 138–40
  trial work period, 143–44
  viatication's noneffect on, 170
  waiting period, 129, 131, 141, 204

women's guideline standards, 143
  See also COBRA
Special enrollment periods, 98
Springing powers of attorney, 48, 208
"Standards for Evaluation of Reasonable Payments" (viatical settlements providers), 181–82
Standby guardians, 43
State HIV/AIDS resources, listing of, 216–30
State laws:
  on creditor-exempt property, 155–56
  "do not resuscitate (DNR) orders" and, 204
  ERISA application to, 118–19
  health insurance provisions, 72, 106, 114–15, 205–6
  HIV-infection as "handicap" status, 186–87
  HIV-related medical expenses funds, 115–16
  insurance incontestability clauses, 73–74
  on licensing viatical settlement providers, 179–80, 209
  living will agent and, 61
  Medicaid mangement and, 133
  mini-COBRA laws and, 106, 207
  1996 federal reform law and, 103–4
  poverty guidelines, 131
  preexisting conditions definitions, 76
  prescription drug coverage, 111
  SSI application procedure, 143
  SSI standards, 138
Stop-loss figure, 93
Student loans, 162, 163
Successor trustee, 24, 25–27, 41, 210
Supplemental Security Income (SSI), 129, 130–32, 138–39
  appeals process, 144–50
  defined, 210

Supplemental Security Income (SSI) (*cont.*)
  limit, 138
  viatication effects on, 170
  See also Medicaid
Survivorship rights, 35–36, 209
Symptoms, keeping record of, 134, 135

Taxable estate, joint property ownership liabilities and, 32, 36–37
Taxes:
  on disability benefits, 85
  exemption from bankruptcy declaration, 162, 163
  viatication proceeds and, 176–77, 209, 210
T-cell count, 133–34, 175
Tenancy in common, 34–35, 36–37, 210
Terminal condition:
  definition of, 60
  do not resuscitate order, 61–62, 204
  living will and, 59–61, 207
Terminally ill individual, definition of, 177–78, 210
Topic-specific resources, list of, 214–16
Trial work period, 143–44
Trustee:
  bankruptcy, 161–63
  living trust, 206
Trusts, 24–28
  appropriateness of, 26–27
  definition, 210
  disadvantages of, 28
  funding of, 25–26
  and incapacity planning, 41
  living, 23–24, 210
  as probate avoidance, 30–31
  successor trustee, 25–26, 27–28, 41

Underwriting, individual, 206
"Undue influence" claims, 23, 64–65, 67, 210–11
  definition, 210–11
Unpaid leave, 198–99, 205

Viatical Association of America (VAA), 172
Viatical Settlements Model Act, 180–81, 182
Viatication, 76–77, 164–84
  accelerated benefits as alternative to, 202
  caveats and pitfalls, 175–76, 183–84
  definition, 211
  legally qualified providers, 179–82, 209
  minimum rates table, 182
  taxability of proceeds, 176–78, 209, 210
  types of companies, 170–74
  workings of, 174
Videotaping, 67

Wage garnishment, 154
Waiver of premium, 76, 83, 204
Will, 15–28
  challenges to, 64–68
  death benefits and, 32–33
  defined, 211
  executor, 18, 204–5, 209, 211
  guardianship of minors provision, 20, 42–43
  importance of, 16–19, 22
  lawyer's help in preparing, 22–23
  notarization of, 16
  probate and, 30, 208–9
  property disposition and, 30, 207
  provisions in, 18–19
  trusts and, 23–28
  "undue influence" claims, 23, 64–65, 67, 210–11
  See also Estate planning; Living will